Emphasizing a Student-Centered Process: Open Pedagogy Course Assessments Across Disciplines

Edited by Angela M. McGowan-Kirsch, PhD and Kelly Soczka Steidinger, M.A.

MILNE OPEN TEXTBOOKS

ISBN: 978-1-956862-14-0

Published by Milne Open Textbooks, Milne Library
State University of New York at Geneseo,
Geneseo, NY 14454

Contents

Acknowledgments

We sincerely thank the many individuals who made this edited volume possible. First and foremost, we are thankful to the contributing authors for their valuable intellectual and pedagogical contributions. Their chapters showcase innovative practices prioritizing student-centered learning and emphasizing the transformative potential of open pedagogy. Thank you, authors, for agreeing to publish your original content under a CC-BY 4.0 license.

We would also like to express our deep appreciation to Christina Hilburger for her invaluable contribution to this project. Her extensive knowledge of open educational resources (OER) and open pedagogy greatly enriched the development of the introduction and conclusion. We deeply appreciate her support and guidance throughout this process.

We extend our sincere gratitude to Sarah Adams, Open Education Librarian at the University of Calgary; Abby Ferrell, Communication Instructor at Mid-State Technical College; and Donna Langille, Community Engagement and Open Education Librarian at the University of British Columbia, Okanagan Campus. Their instrumental contributions as peer reviewers of this text strengthened its clarity, accessibility, and pedagogical impact. We deeply appreciate the time, care, and expertise they brought to the review process.

We also thank our students, whose contributions—through examples, images, and feedback—helped refine and enhance the chapters. We extend a special thanks to Dr. Jean Hertzberg and her student, Jillian Weber, for creating the captivating image, *Watercolors diffuse on a mirror,* which graces the cover of our book. Jillian's image is an exceptional example of how openly licensed materials can enrich educational resources and inspire creative expression. Together, these efforts advance open pedagogy in higher education, promoting inclusivity, diversity, and equity in assessment and engagement.

To Allison Brown, our editor at Milne Publishing, your enthusiasm for this project and expert guidance throughout the publishing process have been instrumental in shaping this work. We also sincerely appreciate the financial support from The State University of New York at Fredonia, which helped bring this book to fruition.

Finally, we thank all those who are engaging with this resource. We hope our collection will inspire you to embrace open pedagogy and create more inclusive, equitable, and student-driven learning environments.

About the Book

Emphasizing a Student-Centered Process: Open Pedagogy Course Assessments Across Disciplines showcases how Open Educational Practices (OEP) empower students as active contributors to knowledge creation. Grounded in constructivist principles, this collection highlights student-centered assessments—from collaborative course design and renewable assignments to generative artificial intelligence—that foster critical thinking, active learning, and inclusivity. Through practical examples and reflective discussions, the book provides educators with actionable strategies to integrate open pedagogical practices across disciplines while addressing challenges such as institutional support, professional development, and resource accessibility.

This publication was made possible through Open Fredonia, with generous financial support from the Daniel A. Reed Library and the Carnahan Jackson Fund for the Humanities, the Office of the Provost at The State University of New York at Fredonia through the SUNY Student Retention Grant, and SUNY OER Services through the 2023 Impact Grant. Their collective commitment to open education enabled the creation and dissemination of this work. We extend our heartfelt gratitude for their invaluable support.

Preface

In recent years, Open Educational Resources (OER) has gained significant traction in higher education as an alternative to traditional textbooks and educational materials. OER refers to openly licensed educational materials—often through Creative Commons licenses—that allow for free access, reuse, modification, and redistribution without needing permission from the copyright holder (Butcher, 2015; D'Antoni, 2009; DeRosa & Robison, 2017). These resources encompass "learning, teaching and research materials in any format and medium that reside in the public domain or are under copyright that have been released under an open license," granting no-cost access and flexibility for adaptation and redistribution (United Nations Educational, Scientific, & Cultural Organization [UNESCO], 2022, p. 9). OER's adaptability allows the content to be tailored to diverse needs, increasing access and elevating collaboration (Wiley & Hilton, 2018). Accordingly, the OER movement represents a shift toward democratizing education.

While the degree of openness varies, it consistently minimizes restrictions and expands opportunities for learners to co-create, share, and peer-review resources (Wiley, 2015). As discussed in Chapters 1 to 5, higher learning institutions are well-positioned to support sustaining open pedagogy practices and stimulating a student-centered, collaborative learning culture. This book explores how educators integrate OER into open pedagogy to transform students from passive consumers to co-creators of learning materials. The five chapters in this text highlight how these practices nurture inclusive, peer-to-peer learning by linking OER with pedagogical innovation.

As intertwined concepts, OER and Open Educational Practices (OEP) can reshape how educators and students engage with knowledge. Encompassing the practices associated with using OER and adopting open pedagogy, OEP emphasizes learner-driven education and positions students as active contributors to knowledge creation (DeRosa & Jhangiani, 2018). While OER typically provides the resources, OEP incorporates them into pedagogical practices that boost collaboration, innovation, and inclusivity. The rise of OEP marks a transition from focusing on acquiring resources to embracing pedagogical practices that position students as active participants in knowledge construction (Koseoglu & Bozkurt, 2018). This evolution supports the belief that OER and OEP provide a pedagogical framework that values students as contributors to the learning process.

As detailed in Chapter 5, open pedagogy also depends on institutional strategies prioritizing faculty and student engagement. Universities can provide critical support by embedding OER and OEP practices in professional development programs and recognizing open pedagogy in promotion and tenure evaluations. By doing so, they create a foundation for sustaining innovative teaching methods while addressing common barriers such as time constraints and resource quality concerns. These institutional commitments are essential for fostering a culture that encourages educators to adopt open pedagogy practices that empower students as co-creators of knowledge.

Building on these ideas, this book examines how OEP and open pedagogy, grounded in constructivist principles, enable faculty to create assessments prioritizing students as content creators. For instance, in Chapters 1 and 4, the authors discuss constructivism and its alignment with OEP and open pedagogy. As a learning theory, constructivism emphasizes the learner's active role in constructing knowledge through meaningful engagement (Fosnot & Perry, 2005). A key principle of constructivism is that learners actively cultivate knowledge (Biggs & Tang, 2011). This principle aligns with OEP and open pedagogy, emphasizing participatory, learner-centered approaches that permit students to co-create and share knowledge in meaningful, community-oriented contexts. By leveraging OER and encouraging transparent, collaborative teaching practices, OEP provides educators with tools to create constructivist learning environments (Cronin & MacLaren, 2018). As Chapters 1 and 4 demonstrate, these practices help educators design active learning experiences that integrate formative feedback, facilitate peer collaboration, and reconstruct students' realities (Hegarty, 2015). Furthermore, OEP mirrors constructivist principles of knowledge construction. The alignment between constructivist theory and OEP underscores a central theme of this book: open pedagogy transforms traditional teaching and learning by promoting environments where learners are not only recipients of knowledge but active contributors to and co-creators in the educational process.

This open pedagogical framework provides the foundation for the authors' design of open pedagogical assessments. It outlines the rationale and boundaries for how open pedagogy redefines traditional learning methods. The book emphasizes how open pedagogy, as a key element of OEP, reshapes education by prioritizing collaboration, critical thinking, and diverse perspectives. The following section examines how open pedagogy transforms learning, highlighting its potential to promote peer learning and equity.

Open Pedagogy: A Cornerstone of OEP

Despite open pedagogy's diverse interpretations (Wiley & Hilton, 2018), there is agreement that open pedagogy emphasizes learning empowerment and positions students as participants in knowledge production (Jhangiani & Green, 2018). Additionally, Hegarty (2015) identified key attributes of open pedagogy that advance a participatory culture and trust among contributors: collaborative technologies, trust, innovation, creativity, and reflective practice. Students become agents of knowledge production while creating and curating content that contributes to the public domain (DeRosa & Robison, 2017). As shown in Chapters 2, 3, and 4, open pedagogy promotes students' creativity by guiding them through the cognitive levels of Bloom's revised taxonomy (Anderson et al., 2000). Its value lies in promoting student agency, skill development, and increasing awareness of open access (Baran & AlZoubi, 2020).

Chapter 1 highlights how the student agency aspect of open pedagogy gives learners choice and control. This, in turn, stimulates connectivity, enhances reflective practices, and promotes engagement (DeRosa & Jhangiani, 2018; Wiley & Hilton, 2018). A key outcome of open pedagogy is the development of student awareness about open access. This occurs as students engage with OER creation, curation, and critical evaluation. As students prepare a resource that others will find helpful, the social and economic impact of open access (D'Antoni, 2009), the ethical considerations in curating and reusing OER (Farrow, 2016), and open licenses (Anderson, 2013). This alignment between open pedagogy and the expansion of student agency underscores the book's focus on transformative learning through enhancing students' abilities to take control of their learning.

Building on the maturation of student agency, open pedagogy also encourages engagement through renewable assignments, which further promote involvement in information creation and the sharing of resources (Wiley, 2013). Renewable assignments, such as those discussed in Chapters 3 and 4, encourage students to produce materials and resources intended for future learners and public use. Student-created OER strengthens learning by preparing content for future students and global learners (Wiley & Hilton, 2018). These assignments differ from disposable assignments that constitute assessments typically only viewed by the instructor and have no further value beyond the classroom (Al Abri & Dabbagh, 2019). According to Wiley (2013), disposable assignments "add no value to the world" (para. 5). In contrast, renewable assessments, such as those discussed in Chapters 2, 3, and 4, encourage students to act as co-creators of knowledge while collaborating with the instructor (Rosen & Smale, 2015). Throughout the book, the authors advocate for assessments that extend beyond traditional boundaries to create lasting value for students, educators, and global learners.

Moreover, open pedagogy, grounded in the principles of OER and OEP, moves beyond providing free and adaptable resources to encouraging active learning. By engaging students as co-creators of knowledge, instructors position students to create renewable assessments emphasizing inclusivity, critical thinking, and problem-solving. As illustrated in Chapters 2, 3, and 4, this participatory approach deepens subject matter understanding and aligns personalizes students' learning experiences. Yet, for faculty to effectively implement the innovative assessments discussed in this book, they need institutional support. As discussed in Chapter 5, colleges and universities can empower educators to design and implement student-centered, impactful assessments by addressing common barriers such as time constraints, coaching, and concerns about resource quality. Equally important is sustaining partnerships across campus that help instructors feel supported in taking pedagogical risks and embracing new approaches that promote diversity, equity, and inclusion.

Role of Open Pedagogy in Fostering Collaboration and Equity

One of the most compelling reasons to embrace OER is its potential to advance diversity and social justice in education (Lambert, 2018). By offering free access to educational resources, OER helps reduce the financial burden on students, especially those from low-income or marginalized communities (Colvard et al., 2018). This accessibility ensures that all students, regardless of their financial background, have an equal opportunity to succeed in their studies. The increasing adoption of OER in U.S. higher education—rising from 6% to 22% in introductory courses between 2017 and 2022—illustrates its growing role in addressing educational inequities (Glapa-Grosskla & Daly, 2023). For instance, OER alleviates textbooks' monetary hurdles while advancing a social justice framework emphasizing access, participation, and empowerment (Lambert, 2018). OER also allows for incorporating diverse perspectives and experiences, which can be crucial for students who may feel alienated by traditional textbooks that often fail to represent their individuality.

OER aligns with the principles of recognitive justice and representational justice (Lambert, 2018); consequently, as educators advance the open education movement, they endorse a belief that all students should have access to an education that reflects their unique identities and experiences. Recognitive justice emphasizes the acknowledgment and respect for cultural and gender differences. In contrast, representational justice ensures that marginalized groups can voice their perspectives and see themselves reflected in educational content. For instance, research indicates that open pedagogy allows marginalized groups to co-construct texts and share their stories (Lambert, 2018). By incorporating open pedagogy, educators offer students the chance to engage with materials that represent diverse cultural, racial, gender, and social experiences. This pedagogical practice, in turn, enhances a more inclusive and respectful learning environment. This book builds on these ideas, exploring how educators use OER and OEP to create inclusive, collaborative, and transformative learning environments where students access and actively contribute knowledge.

References

Al Abri, M. H., & Dabbagh, N. (2019). Testing the intervention of OER renewable assignments in a college course. *Open Praxis, 11*(2), 195-209. https://doi.org/10.5944/openpraxis.11.2.916

Anderson, L., Krathwohl, D., Airasian, P., Cruikshank, K., Mayer, R., Pintrich, P., Raths, J., & Wittrock, M. (2000). *Taxonomy for learning, teaching, and assessing: A revision of Bloom's Taxonomy of Educational Objectives.* Pearson.

Anderson, T. (2013). Open access scholarly publications as OER. *The International Review of Research in Open and Distributed Learning, 14*(2), 81–95. https://doi.org/10.19173/irrodl.v14i2.1531

Baran, E., & AlZoubi, D. (2020). Affordances, challenges, and impact of open pedagogy: Examining students' voices. *Distance Education, 41*(2), 230-244. https://doi.org/10.1080/01587919.2020.1757409

Biggs, J. B., & Tang, C. (2011). *Teaching for quality learning at university* (4th ed.). Society for Research into Higher Education & Open University Press.

Butcher, N. (2015). *A basic guide to open educational resources (OER).* (A. Kanwar & S. Uvalic-Trumbic, Eds.). United Nations Educational, Scientific, and Cultural Organization. https://unesdoc.unesco.org/ark:/48223/pf0000215804

Colvard, N. B., Watson, C. E., & Park, H. (2018). The impact of open educational resources on various student success metrics. *International Journal of Teaching and Learning in Higher Education, 30*(2), 262-276. https://files.eric.ed.gov/fulltext/EJ1184998.pdf

Cronin, C., & MacLaren, I. (2018). Conceptualising OEP: A review of theoretical and empirical literature on open educational practices. *Open Praxis, 10*(2), 127-143. https://doi.org/10.5944/openpraxis.10.2.825

D'Antoni, S. (2009). Open educational resources: Reviewing initiatives and issues. *Open Learning: The Journal of Open, Distance and e-Learning, 24*(1), 3–10. https://doi.org/10.1080/02680510802625443

DeRosa, R., & Jhangiani, R. (2018). Open pedagogy. In Rebus Community (Ed.), *A guide to making open textbooks with students.* Pressbooks. https://press.rebus.community/makingopentextbookswithstudents/chapter/open-pedagogy

DeRosa, R., & Robison, S. (2017). From OER to open pedagogy: Harnessing the power of open. In R.S. Jhangiani and R. Biswas-Diener (Eds.), *Open: The philosophy and practices that are revolutionizing education and science* (pp. 115-124). Ubiquity Press. https://doi.org/10.5334/bbc.i

Ehlers, U. D. (2011). Extending the territory: From open educational resources to open educational practices. *Journal of Open, Flexible, and Distance Learning, 15*(2), 1–10. https://www.learntechlib.org/p/147891/

Farrow, R. (2016). A framework for the ethics of open education. *Open Praxis, 8*(2), 93–109. https://www.learntechlib.org/p/173546/

Fosnot, C. T., & Perry, R. S. (2005). Constructivism: A psychological theory of learning. In C.T. Fosnot (Ed.), *Constructivism: Theory, perspectives, and practice* (pp. 8– 38). Teachers College Press.

Glapa-Grosskla, J. & Daly, U. (2023, April 27). The future of open educational resources. *American Association of Community Colleges: Community College Daily.* https://www.ccdaily.com/2023/04/the-future-of-open-educational-resources/

Hegarty, B. (2015). Attributes of open pedagogy: A model for using open educational resources. *Educational Technology, 55*(4), 3–13. http://www.jstor.org/stable/44430383

Hilton, J. (2020). Open educational resources, student efficacy, and user perceptions: A synthesis of research published between 2015 and 2018. *Educational Technology Research and Development, 68*, 853-876. https://doi.org/10.1007/s11423-019-09700-4

Jhangiani, R. S. & Green, A. G. (2018). An open athenaeum: Creating an institutional home for open pedagogy. In A. Wesolek, J. Lashley, & A. Langley (Eds.), *OER: A field guide for academic librarians* (pp. 141–161). Pacific University Press. https://boisestate.pressbooks.pub/oer-field-guide/chapter/an-open-athenaeum-creating-an-institutional-home-for-open-pedagogy/

Koseoglu, S., & Bozkurt, A. (2018). An exploratory literature review on open educational practices. *Distance Education, 39*(4), 441–461. https://doi.org/10.1080/01587919.2018.1520042

Lambert, S. R. (2018). Changing our (dis)course: A distinctive social justice aligned definition of open education. *Journal of Learning for Development, 5*(3), 225-244. https://doi.org/10.56059/jl4d.v5i3.290

Rosen, J. R., & Smale, M. A. (2015). Open digital pedagogy = Critical pedagogy. *Hybrid Pedagogy*. https://hybridpedagogy.org/open-digital-pedagogy-critical-pedagogy/

United Nations Educational, Scientific, and Cultural Organization. (2022). *The 2019 UNESCO recommendation on Open Education Resources (OER)*. https://unesdoc.unesco.org/ark:/48223/pf0000383205/PDF/383205eng.pdf.multi

Wiley, D. (2013, October 21). What is open pedagogy? *Improving Learning: Eclectic, Pragmatic, Enthusiastic*. https://opencontent.org/blog/archives/2975

Wiley, D. (2015, January 31). Open pedagogy: The importance of getting in the air. *Improving Learning: Eclectic, Pragmatic, Enthusiastic*. https://opencontent.org/blog/archives/3761

Wiley, D., & Hilton III, J. L. (2018). Defining OER-enabled pedagogy. *The International Review of Research in Open and Distributed Learning, 19*(4), 133-147. https://doi.org/10.19173/irrodl.v19i4.3601

Overview of the Book

Although the literature indicates positive attitudes toward open educational resources (OER) among students and instructors (Hilton, 2020), adopting OER in educational contexts has often been slower than anticipated (Ehlers, 2011). This highlights the need to explore further strategies to integrate OER into teaching practices across disciplines. The chapters in this volume argue that by incorporating these practices, instructors can intellectually challenge students, propel critical thinking, and encourage greater investment in learning. Specifically, the book posits that students become more deeply engaged when they take ownership of their learning by contributing to course design and applying course concepts to real-world scenarios. An underlying theme is that this approach produces analytical thinking and helps students understand the relevance of their learning.

Emphasizing a Student-Centered Process: Open Pedagogy Course Assessments Across Disciplines illustrates how open pedagogy can create meaningful, inclusive, and collaborative learning environments. Grounded in both theory and practice, the book's five chapters showcase diverse approaches to student-centered learning, with each contributor offering pedagogical strategies that emphasize collaboration, transparency, and real-world application.

Chapter 1, by Hether, establishes the book's foundation by examining how students co-create syllabi and assignments in an upper-division communication course. Her emphasis on collaboration and curriculum design reflects the core goals of open pedagogy, namely fostering student ownership, critical thinking, and long-term relevance. This approach sets the stage for later chapters by demonstrating how open practices can be embedded in the structural design of a course.

Chapters 2 and 3 extend open pedagogy into disciplinary contexts where it is less commonly applied. In Chapter 2, Hertzberg explores a flow visualization course in engineering, where students use artistic expression to represent fluid dynamics. By incorporating oral critiques and public sharing of creative work, she highlights the role of creativity and visibility in student learning. Chapter 3, by Lohiser, focuses on observational research in an interdisciplinary course for non-scientists. Students use EarthCam and OERs to develop essential research skills, aligning with Bloom's taxonomy and demonstrating how open pedagogy can foster higher-order thinking. Together, these chapters illustrate how open pedagogy encourages both creative and scientific engagement, supporting learners with varied academic backgrounds.

Chapters 4 and 5 broaden the lens of open pedagogy. In Chapter 4, Steidinger introduces a renewable assessment in which students evaluate and revise AI-generated multiple-choice questions. This practice advances students' critical thinking and promotes ethical engagement with emerging technologies while also creating useful resources for future learners. In

Chapter 5, Hilburger shifts to an institutional perspective by detailing a campus-wide model for supporting open pedagogy through infrastructure and collaboration. This chapter underscores the importance of administrative support in sustaining and scaling open practices.

Following the authors' contributions, McGowan-Kirsch will reflect on the key insights from this volume, emphasizing the transformative potential of open pedagogy and OEP. Throughout the five chapters, the authors illustrate how these practices can foster collaboration and enhance critical thinking by making students active participants in learning. I will also discuss how these open pedagogy practices create more equitable learning environments by promoting diverse voices and perspectives. The book concludes by exploring the implications of open pedagogy.

Taken together, the chapters in this volume reveal the multifaceted nature of open pedagogy. From course-level design to institution-wide frameworks, and from creative expression to research-based skill building, the book illustrates how open pedagogy empowers students as active participants in their education. These contributions collectively highlight the potential of open educational practices to foster equity, innovation, and lasting engagement across disciplines.

1. The Collaborative Syllabus: Empowering Students as Co-creators of their Learning Experience

Heather J. Hether, PhD

Chapter Learning Objectives:

- Explain how a collaborative syllabus is illustrative of open pedagogy.
- Identify how a collaborative syllabus can support student learning.
- List the potential benefits and challenges of a collaborative syllabus.
- Describe the steps to implement a collaborative syllabus.

Chapter Overview

Open pedagogy goes beyond integrating open educational resources (OER) into a course. Instead, it is an approach that can influence every aspect of instructional activity, including course design. This chapter describes how students in an upper division communication course, *Social Media for Public Relations*, participated in course design through a collaborative syllabus. The collaborative syllabus is a practice that reflects learner-centered teaching, supports social justice, and empowers students. While there are some challenges associated with it, with clear structure and intentional planning it can be a productive activity that serves as a gateway to open pedagogy.

1. How are you engaging and empowering your students in their learning?
2. How can you make your courses more dynamic such that they respond to each unique cohort of students?
3. How would your students respond to an invitation to participate in course design?
4. How can you leverage a collaborative syllabus to support a more inclusive learning experience for your students?

Rationale

In learner-centered teaching, instructors are learning facilitators and students are empowered with agency and influence over their learning experience (Weimer, 2013). This is a model of teaching, reflected in a variety of instructional strategies, which can infuse the classroom experience with energy and excitement and facilitate learning at higher levels (Froyd & Simpson, 2008). For instructors committed to learner-centered teaching, open pedagogy has an inherent appeal. As a learner-centered approach, open pedagogy diverges from a traditional model of instruction by decentering the instructor and empowering students more strongly in their learning.

One way to make a course more learner-centered is to involve students in its design. A variety of tactics can support collaborative course design, including a collaborative syllabus (Aiken et al., 2017). Working together, a collaborative syllabus decenters the instructor by inviting students into course design. In this activity, the term begins with a tentative or partially complete syllabus and students are invited to contribute their ideas to course design.

A collaborative syllabus is an open pedagogy practice – the syllabus is open for student input, which will influence their learning experience (DeRosa & Robison, 2017). For instructors seeking to adopt open pedagogy, a collaborative syllabus is a learner-centered activity that aligns with the values of open pedagogy, including its emphasis on social justice. Moreover, a collaborative syllabus can be a gateway instructional activity that can ease a learning community toward more openness without overwhelming faculty or students.

Learner-Centered Teaching

Learner-centered teaching is an approach to teaching that shifts the focus away from how an instructor *teaches* to a focus on how students *learn* (Smart et al., 2012). More than semantics, this shift has practical implications in the classroom. Instead of focusing on what the instructor is doing to transmit knowledge to students, this approach focuses on what students can do (guided by instructional strategies) to learn new knowledge. Weimer (2013) identifies five characteristics of learner-centered teaching that holistically focus on engaging, motivating, and empowering students through collaboration, reflection, and skills development.

Learner-centered teaching is an instructional approach that is informed by several pedagogical and learning theories, including constructivism (Weimer, 2013). Constructivism is a seminal learning theory premised on the notion that the learner does not passively receive knowledge from the instructor. Instead, learners construct knowledge and develop insights through reconciling new information with existing understanding (Fosnot & Perry, 2005).

Constructivism is associated with a range of instructional practices that typically include active learning. Active learning refers to learning by experience or doing things in the classroom (as opposed to at home). Active learning is usually contrasted with learning through listening to lectures, which is seen as passive (Misseyanni et al., 2018; Prince, 2004). For example, Smart et al. (2012) used what they called a "KWL approach" (p. 394) to engage students in learning a new theory. In this approach, when learning a new theory relative to a topic, students are first asked 1) what they know, 2) what they want to learn, and 3) what they learned (captured after the lesson). The authors use this activity to better understand what students know about a topic and to facilitate questions. The work of Bain (2004) was informative in this study for its description of what learners do when they encounter new information, which is, "[learners] try to comprehend it in terms of something [they] already know" (p. 26). Bain explains how existing mental models shape how learners take in new information, which often leads to a very different understanding than what was intended. Thus, identifying what students already know about a topic is helpful in understanding how they might learn new information. Smart et al.'s (2012) activity reflects active learning, anchored in constructivist learning theory.

While the collaborative syllabus does not directly facilitate student learning of new material, it does lay the foundation for forthcoming learning. Through this activity, which was integrated into a communication course: *Social Media for Public Relations*, students reflect on what they know, what they do not know (or would like to know more about), how they would like to learn, and how they would like to demonstrate their learning. It is learner-centered because it allows students to contribute to the course's "learning agenda" (Weimer, 2013, p.15). In addition, this activity incorporates both individual reflection and collaboration, a practice supported by constructivism and learner-centered teaching.

By asking students what they would like to learn and how they would like to learn it, the collaborative syllabus creates a bridge between what students already know to what they don't know but would like to learn more about. By working through this activity, first individually and then collaboratively, students are not limited to their own individual understanding. This activity lays the foundation for a constructivist approach to learning by providing a framework for students to assimilate new knowledge into their current understanding (Bain, 2004; Weimer, 2013). Moreover, it provides agency to students by asking for their input on what activities help them learn and how they would like to demonstrate their learning.

Encouraging student agency is reflective of learner-centered teaching, as well as open pedagogy. Indeed, as a learner-centered approach, open pedagogy relies on reflection, collaboration, and skills development. Moreover, open pedagogy pushes the notion of learner-centered teaching even further by adding another layer of "student-centeredness" into its perspective: a commitment to social justice and its core values of access and inclusiveness. Similarly, the collaborative syllabus is an activity that can be leveraged to support these values, too.

Open Pedagogy and Social Justice

A key characteristic of open pedagogy is its embrace of diverse cultural voices as design partners (Tietjien & Asino, 2021), emphasizing collaboration among various course elements and stakeholders. A truly participatory and collaborative course must be inclusive, empowering students, especially from marginalized communities, and fostering a more equitable learning environment (Bali et al., 2020; Clinton-Lisell, 2021). A collaborative syllabus can support social justice by inviting all student voices into course design through individual and collective participation. By encouraging students to reflect on the syllabus, share their opinions with the instructor, and collaborate with classmates to develop joint recommendations, the course can become more inclusive. Thoughtful management of class discussions allows the instructor to identify areas of disagreement and encourage a diversity of opinions, further enriching the learning experience.

Indeed, welcoming diverse student voices into course design is an important part of the collaborative syllabus activity. By working together on Day One of the course, we establish a culture of openness, trust, and collaboration (key attributes of open pedagogy) that will undergird the entire course (Hegarty, 2015). Moreover, this activity can be as large or as discrete as an instructor feels comfortable. As such, it offers a manageable first step for instructors who want to wade into open pedagogy without overwhelming themselves or their students.

Gateway to Open Pedagogy

While discussions of open pedagogy often focus on open educational resources (OER), its reach extends far beyond informing all aspects of instruction. A widely referenced framework by Nascimbeni and Burgos (2016) outlines the Open Educator concept, which integrates openness into an educator's roles in design, content, pedagogy, and assessment. Open course design can involve sharing curricula and co-designing courses with instructors and students, while open course content embraces a variety of sources beyond the instructor, including

OERs. Open pedagogy emphasizes teaching practices that foster the co-creation of knowledge through collaboration and content creation with students, and open assessment expands traditional methods to include peer assessment and other innovative approaches. Collaborative syllabus-building exemplifies open course design by inviting students to contribute to the course's learning architecture (DeRosa & Jhangiani, n.d.), engaging them as active participants in its development (Aiken et al., 2017). Research indicates that involving students in collaborative course design leads to increased perceived learning, higher course satisfaction, and improved professor evaluations (Aiken et al., 2017; Downing et al., 2018; Jafar, 2016).

Nascimbeni and Burgos (2016) identify various pathways to openness in higher education while noting that it is not the default approach for instructors; rather, it requires intentional development. They propose a three-stage process for instructors to enhance their capacity for openness, starting with awareness, progressing to fluency, and ultimately achieving openness as a default practice. The collaborative syllabus plays a role in this journey by supporting instructors in developing fluency with open pedagogy. It serves as an initial step toward open course design, allowing instructors to customize the level of student input based on their comfort and readiness. As instructors build their capacity for openness, the collaborative syllabus can expand in complexity and depth, making it a flexible approach suited to both instructors and their students.

The collaborative syllabus provides an opportunity to integrate both the values of open pedagogy (Werth & Williams, 2022) and the principles of learner-centered teaching (Weimer, 2013) into the fabric of course design. Moreover, it is a manageable activity that helps develop fluency with open approaches because not every element of the syllabus has to be fully open. Pre-established course learning outcomes must continue to be supported. However, in an upper division course whose subject matter is dynamic and also oriented toward participation and engagement, such as a course on social media, the collaborative syllabus is a worthwhile activity.

Assessment Description

While higher education typically emphasizes summative assessments—assessments that occur at the end of a learning module or course that ultimately contribute to final course grades—the collaborative syllabus serves as a tool for formative assessment (Wheatley et al., 2015). Formative assessment includes "those activities undertaken by teachers, and/or by their students, which provide information to be used as feedback to modify the teaching and learning activities in which they are engaged" (Black & William, 1998, p. 8). Indeed, the collaborative syllabus is an activity that yields formative assessment data on students' current understanding of the topic and where they feel there are gaps in their learning that the course can or should address. In addition, the collaborative syllabus provides an opportunity to seek student feedback on summative assessments—how they think they can best demonstrate their learning. As a formative assessment, though, it is not necessary to apply an assessment rubric or grade to this activity.

A four-step process outlined in Table 1, modeled on earlier scholarship (i.e., Aiken et al., 2016; Jafar, 2016; Kaplan & Renard, 2015; Murray, 2021), describes how this activity was applied in an upper division course. These steps include:

1. presenting a "tentative" syllabus to students on Day One of the course;
2. soliciting student feedback through individual reflection, collaborative group work, and whole class discussion;
3. integrating student feedback into course design, as appropriate, and
4. sharing the modified syllabus with students during the second week of the term.
5. An additional step that brings the process full circle is using the annotated syllabus to structure a final review during the last class.

By following this process, described in detail below, students are invited to invest and engage in the course by suggesting how it can best meet their needs.

Table 1: Four-step Process to a Collaborative Syllabus.

Step	Who?	What?	When?	Where?	How long?
1.	Instructor	Present "tentative" syllabus to students for their feedback.	First class	In class	20 minutes
2.	Students	Provide feedback to the instructor through individual reflection, group work, and full-class discussion.	First class	In class	1 hour
3.	Instructor	Analysis and integration of student feedback into syllabus, as appropriate.	Week 1	Out of class	2 hours
4.	Instructor	Share annotated final syllabus with students indicating changes made.	Week 2	In class	20 minutes

Context

The course, *Social Media for Public Relations,* is an advanced public relations course in which students learn the theories and practices that guide effective social media planning and implementation in the context of organizational public relations. The course is set in the context of a large public university, with a typical class size of 40-50 students.

This course can be challenging to teach because of the dynamic nature of its subject matter. While the course is anchored in theory and research related to effective social media practice, because of the ever-changing social media landscape, course materials are continually evolving. Moreover, this course confronts student expectations that are influenced by their own personal and pre-professional experience with social media, as well as their future career aspirations. In other words, students come to the course with a lot of "hands-on" experience with social media in terms of both production and consumption, and they often have specific career interests that motivate them to take this course.

Thus, because this is an advanced course predominately taken by seniors, students are far enough along into their education to identify (to some degree) what they know and what they do not know and would like to learn more about (i.e., conscious competence and conscious incompetence) (Burch, 1970). This makes this course, along with its subject matter that is also predicated on engagement and participation, particularly suitable for a collaborative syllabus.

Activity

This activity begins on the first day of class after students are welcomed and introduced to the instructor, their peers, and the course topic. The instructor presents a tentative syllabus. How tentative (or open) the syllabus is varies, as deemed appropriate by the instructor to facilitate course learning outcomes. For example, some theories, topics, or assessments might be "non-negotiable," whereas others might be more flexible.

Once the syllabus is introduced and its "in progress" status is explained, the instructor invites student contributions to the syllabus. Student contributions are facilitated in class through individual and collaborative participation. Firstly, inspired by earlier work (e.g., Aiken et al., 2016), students are individually asked to write answers to these three questions:

1. What would you like to learn?
2. What kinds of assignments help you learn best?
3. What is your Big Question? (see Appendix A).

This part of the process typically takes around 10 minutes. As needed, student feedback can also be solicited on other relevant issues, such as the most appropriate channel for office hours (face-to-face or Zoom) and more targeted questions related to assessment, if appropriate, such as determining the preferred graded weight of exams to papers. At the end of class, individual responses are collected by the instructor.

After time is provided for individual reflection, students are then assigned to small groups and asked to compare their perspectives. As a group, they synthesize the individual perspectives into one cohesive response to the questions and write them on a large, adhesive-backed note paper, which is then posted on the wall (see Appendix B). Next, the instructor facilitates a whole-class discussion by moving through each group's response, looking for similarities and differences, and making connections with the existing syllabus. Altogether, this small group and whole-class discussion can take approximately one hour. Although, the amount of time it takes varies based on the prompts, how much of the syllabus is open, and how much class time the instructor has available to commit to it. The instructor photographs and collects these large, sticky note papers at the end of class.

After the first class, the instructor compares the individual responses submitted by students and their collective responses with the tentative syllabus. The instructor does this work outside of class, preferably between Week One and Two. First, the instructor organizes the individual student feedback and conducts both a quantitative analysis of it (i.e., how many students responded in a particular way) and a qualitative, thematic analysis of it. Then, these analyses, as well as the collaborative responses, are compared to the tentative syllabus. Once the feedback is analyzed, the instructor decides how to most effectively integrate it into the syllabus.

In reviewing student feedback, the instructor can modify the course schedule to include topics suggested by students, or they may determine that some topics suggested by students are outside the scope of the course. Likewise, the instructor can decide how and where to integrate student feedback about the preferred learning activities and assessments. To keep the class on schedule, this analysis and its related syllabus adjustments should be made before the second week of class.

By the second week of class, the instructor shares the analyses of the individual and group feedback with students. For this process, an annotated syllabus is helpful because it can indicate how the original, tentative syllabus already aligned with student interests, in addition to showing how the syllabus was modified in response to student feedback. This presentation finalizes the syllabus, and the course proceeds as designed.

The last optional step of this activity brings this process full circle when, at the end of the term, the feedback solicited from students on Day One is used to frame a review of the entire course. This provides an opportunity to reiterate the educational value of the course and how it was planned collaboratively with students to meet their needs and interests. This is a positive way to end the term and resituates students at the center of their learning experience. Moreover, it is also an effective way to show how course content supported course learning outcomes.

Debrief

I have integrated this activity twice into the same upper division social media course. Overall, it is an engaging practice with which to start a school term that yields formative assessment data, invites students into the course as co-creators (Campbell, 2022; Hudd, 2003; Jafar, 2016), and sets expectations for student participation and collaboration. Moreover, this activity can take up as much or as little time as appropriate and remains a valuable exercise.

In my applications of this activity, I have varied the scope of student contributions to the syllabus, given other priorities I may have had for students that term. For example, the first time I integrated the collaborative syllabus after the pandemic, I invited student feedback on the topics addressed in the course and the assessment plan. I had decided on the overall structure of assessments (a mixture of low-stakes quizzes and applied activities, along with exams and longer written work). Still, I invited student suggestions regarding the graded weight of the larger assignments and exams and the ratio of exams relative to the written work. Thus, I asked students during the initial exercise, "What is the best way for you to demonstrate your learning in this course?" In class, we discussed the various potential options. After receiving student feedback, I changed the variety and scope of the assignments, which included adding another midterm exam and another shorter writing assignment.

The second time I applied this activity, I had already reorganized course assignments and integrated a new assignment in response to the increasing prevalence of generative AI. Therefore, I did not solicit student feedback on summative assessment methods; instead, student feedback was centered on course topics and identifying activities that support student learning. After receiving student feedback, which expressed an interest in career and professional skills development, I modified the course schedule and added two guest speaker lectures. Making this change illustrates how the course is enhanced by student feedback and demonstrates how students can influence their learning experience.

It is important to note that this activity is effective at initiating dialogue and cultivating a student-centered environment; however, it does not mean the instructor has to forfeit their role as the subject matter and pedagogical expert. Ultimately, the instructor has to make the final decisions related to course content, assessment, and scheduling. Still, this activity fosters a more democratic process whereby the instructor demonstrates they are listening to students and that students' perspectives matter.

Ultimately, students are diverse, and this process does not guarantee that all students' needs and interests are addressed. Still, it provides an opportunity for the instructor to acknowledge them. For example, the second time I did this activity, a student expressed interest in learning about monetizing social media platforms—i.e., generating revenue as an influencer or content creator. However, monetization is outside the course's scope and the instructor's expertise. Therefore, while I shared this student's interest with the class, I explained how we would not explicitly address it due to the reasons already mentioned. Yet, throughout the term, where there were learning opportunities that connected with monetization, I certainly highlighted that for students in an ongoing effort to address this interest.

This activity is designed to be inclusive and welcoming of diverse student perspectives—through both individual and collective feedback. Admittedly, while all students are encouraged to voice their perspectives, there is still a chance that students may hold back their genuine opinions in the group discussion. However, with intentional and supportive discussion facilitation, the instructor can tease out any intra-or cross-group disagreements and minority opinions. Moreover, a lack of consensus provides a great opportunity for a deeper discussion. In this upper division class, though, students are typically more comfortable voicing contrarian opinions than students in lower division classes and these diverse opinions tend to be appreciated by peers.

While this activity has the potential to be a renewable assignment, according to the typology of OER-enabled pedagogy (Wiley & Hilton, 2018), it has not yet reached the level of OER in this course. Instead, it is an authentic assignment: "it has value beyond supporting its creator's learning" (Wiley & Hilton, 2018, p. 137). In this course, the collaborative syllabus supports individual and peer learning, thus making it authentic. While each co-created syllabus from one course term informs the tentative syllabus for the following cohort of students, it is not a renewable assignment because it has not been shared more broadly.

Appraisal

The collaborative syllabus works well in an upper division course. It is a learner-centered activity that conveys expectations to students about participation and collaboration, provides a formative assessment of students' knowledge about the topic, and invites students into the course as co-creators. Moreover, it is anchored in constructivist learning theory, supports social justice values, and can provide a gateway to open pedagogy. Despite these benefits, there can also be some challenges with this activity.

Foremost, it requires time to integrate into the course schedule since it is an in-class activity. Thus, it is important for the instructor to be realistic about the time they have to devote to the collaborative syllabus and the scope of feedback they can realistically apply to course design. It works well as an activity for the first week of class because it is a nice way to introduce students to the course and slowly accelerate their learning. Moreover, since this activity shifts the traditional roles of instructor and students, it requires the instructor to cede some control over the course structure. However, this can be mitigated by slowly opening up only parts of the syllabus to student input as the instructor gains fluency with this approach (i.e., Nascimbeni & Burgos, 2016). Lastly, this activity may work better with upper level students because it relies on students having some understanding of the subject matter and metacognition related to how they learn best. Students must know what they don't know (i.e., conscious incompetence) to identify topics they would like to know more about (i.e., Burch, 1970). Lower level students may not be able to participate in this and, consequently, they may be overwhelmed (Jafar, 2016). Therefore, there can be challenges with implementing this activity, yet these can be addressed with thoughtful planning and clearly communicated expectations.

Thus far, in my application of this activity, I have been fairly conservative with the scope of student input on the syllabus. Through this activity, I have sought student feedback on course topics, assignments, and assessments, and their feedback has influenced course design. However, the course is very much co-created with me and I have not left critical aspects of course design solely up to students. This ensures the course remains aligned with learning outcomes and supports student learning through effective pedagogy.

In future applications, I would like to open the course up even further by integrating more student feedback across more course elements. For example, beyond the essential course learning outcomes, students can be asked to identify one or two more that they would like to achieve. In addition, students can be asked to identify how the course could be more inclusive in its design. Practices from Lutz et al. (2021) that focus on inclusive design, delivery, and assessment can be shared with students for their consideration in the syllabus. These practices include diverse theoretical perspectives and researchers, presenting materials in diverse formats, and using multiple assessment methods. Opening this course to more student input will further support student learning through increased opportunities for student agency, active learning, and metacognition (see Stanton et al., 2021).

Moving forward, identifying how this activity could be made into a renewable assignment deserves some attention, too. This syllabus could be shared more broadly with other learning communities that could also build on it. Moreover, this activity could be expanded within the context of this course to include a historical perspective wherein students compare their interests and feedback to past cohorts. This could potentially provide an informal trend analysis that could further extend student learning.

Another potential iteration is to leverage this activity more systematically and comprehensively as a benchmark for student learning. For example, at the beginning of the course, students could be asked to reflect upon one aspect of course design, such as topics they think are important to address and why. Students could then respond to a similar prompt as a summative assessment at the end of the course. This comparative reflection would demonstrate how their understanding, analysis, and evaluation have changed over the duration of the course.

Summary

Open pedagogy represents a transformative shift in higher education, empowering students to take greater agency in their learning by contributing to course design, collaborating with peers, and engaging in assessments in new ways. This modern approach necessitates a re-conceptualization of roles for both instructors and students. Recognizing that significant changes in established institutions take time, the chapter highlights the collaborative syllabus as a valuable entry point into this new educational paradigm, enabling both students and instructors to embark on their journey toward open pedagogy while achieving various instructional goals.

References

Aiken, K. D., Heinze, T. C., Meuter, M. L., & Chapman, K. J. (2016). Innovation through collaborative course development: Theory and practice. *Marketing Education Review, 26*(1), 57-62. https://doi.org/10.1080/10528008.2015.1091679

Aiken, K.D., Heinze, T.C., Meuter, M.L., & Chapman, K.J. (2017). The impact of collaboration, empowerment, and choice: An empirical examination of the collaborative course development method. *Marketing Education Review, 27*(1), 39-50. https://doi.org/10.1080/10528008.2016.1255852

Bain, K. (2004). *What the best college teachers do.* Harvard University Press.

Bali, M., Cronin, C., & Jhangiani, R. S. (2020). Framing open educational practices from a social justice perspective. *Journal of Interactive Media in Education, 1*(10), 1-12. https://doi.org/10.5334/jime.565

Black, P., & William, D. (1998). Assessment and classroom learning. *Assessment in Education: Principles, Policy & Practice, 5*(1), 7–74. https://doi.org/10.1080/0969595980050102

Burch, N. (1970). *The four stages for learning any new skill.* Gordon Training International.

Campbell, L. M. (2022). *Open education and OER in the curriculum.* (Curriculum Transformation Programme). The University of Edinburgh. https://www.docs.hss.ed.ac.uk/iad/Learning_teaching/CTP/OER_in_the_Curriculum.pdf

Clinton-Lisell, V. (2021). Open pedagogy: A systematic review of empirical findings. *Journal of Learning for Development, 8*(2), 255-268. https://doi.org/10.56059/jl4d.v8i2.511

DeRosa, R., & Jhangiani, R. (n.d.). *Open pedagogy.* Open Pedagogy Notebook. https://openpedagogy.org/open-pedagogy/

DeRosa R. & Robison S. (2017). From OER to open pedagogy: Harnessing the power of open. In R.S. Jhangiani & R. Biswas-Diener (Eds.), *Open: The philosophy and practices that are revolutionizing education and science* (pp. 115-124). Ubiquity Press. https://doi.org/10.5334/bbc.i

Downing, J. A., Aiken, D., McCoy, D., Matthews, M. E., & Deatley, K. (2018). Collaborative course development: A comparison of business and non-business students' perceptions of class experience. *The International Journal of Management Education, 16*(2), 256-265. https://doi.org/10.1016/j.ijme.2018.04.002

Fosnot, C. T., & Perry, R. S. (2005). Constructivism: A psychological theory of learning. In C.T. Fosnot (Ed.), *Constructivism: Theory, perspectives, and practice* (pp. 8– 38). Teachers College Press.

Froyd J., & Simpson N. (2008). *Student-centered learning addressing faculty questions about student centered learning* [Conference session]. Course, Curriculum, Labor, and Improvement Conference, Washington, DC, United States.

Hegarty, B. (2015). Attributes of open pedagogy: A model for using open educational resources. *Educational Technology, 55*(4), 3-13. https://www.jstor.org/stable/44430383

Hudd, S. S. (2003). Syllabus under construction: Involving students in the creation of class assignments. *Teaching Sociology, 31*(2), 195-202. https://doi.org/10.2307/3211308

Jafar, A. (2016). Student engagement, accountability, and empowerment: A case study of collaborative course design. *Teaching Sociology, 44*(3), 221-232. https://doi.org/10.1177/0092055X16644489

Kaplan, D. M., & Renard, M. K. (2015). Negotiating your syllabus: Building a collaborative contract. *Journal of Management Education, 39*(3), 400-421. https://doi.org/10.1177/1052562914564788

Lutz, C., Untaru, L., & van Goch, M. (2021, July). Developing a shared syllabus template as a living document of inclusive practices in a teaching and learning community. In *7th International Conference on Higher Education Advances (HEAd'21)* (pp. 481-489). Editorial Universitat Politècnica de València. http://dx.doi.org/10.4995/HEAd21.2021.12967

Misseyanni, A., Papadopoulou, P., Marouli, C., & Lytras, M.D. (2018). Active learning stories in higher education: Lessons learned and good practices in STEM education. In A. Misseyanni, M.D. Lytras, P. Papadopoulo, & C. Marouli (Eds.), *Active learning strategies in higher education: Teaching for leadership, innovation, and creativity* (pp. 75-106). Emerald Publishing. https://doi.org/10.1108/978-1-78714-487-320181004

Murray, M. B. (2021). Collaborative syllabus building: The "buffet-style" career preparation course for dance majors. *Dance Education in Practice, 7*(2), 9-14. https://doi.org/10.1080/23734833.2021.1916287

Nascimbeni, F., & Burgos, D. (2016). In search for the open educator: Proposal of a definition and a framework to increase openness adoption among university educators. *International Review of Research in Open and Distributed Learning, 17*(6), 1-17. https://doi.org/10.19173/irrodl.v17i6.2736

Prince, M. (2004). Does active learning work? A review of the research. *Journal of Engineering Education, 93*(3), 223-231. https://doi.org/10.1002/j.2168-9830.2004.tb00809.x

Smart, K. L., Witt, C., & Scott, J. P. (2012). Toward learner-centered teaching: An inductive approach. *Business Communication Quarterly, 75*(4), 392-403. https://doi.org/10.1177/1080569912459752

Stanton, J. D., Sebesta, A. J., & Dunlosky, J. (2021). Fostering metacognition to support student learning and performance. *CBE—Life Sciences Education, 20*(2), 1-7. https://doi.org/10.1187/cbe.20-12-0289

Tietjen, P., & Asino, T. I. (2021). What is open pedagogy? Identifying commonalities. *International Review of Research in Open and Distributed Learning, 22*(2), 185-204. https://doi.org/10.19173/irrodl.v22i2.5161

Weimer, M. (2013). *Learner-centered teaching: Five key changes to practice.* John Wiley & Sons.

Werth, E., & Williams, K. (2022). The why of open pedagogy: A value-first conceptualization for enhancing instructor praxis. *Smart Learning Environments, 9*(10), 1-22. https://doi.org/10.1186/s40561-022-00191-0

Wheatley, L., Lord, R., McInch, A., & Fleming, S. (2015). Feeding back to feed forward: Formative assessment as a platform for effective learning. *Kentucky Journal of Higher Education Policy and Practice, 3*(2), 1-31. https://uknowledge.uky.edu/kjhepp/vol3/iss2/2/

Wiley, D., & Hilton III, J. L. (2018). Defining OER-enabled pedagogy. *The International Review of Research in Open and Distributed Learning, 19*(4), 133-147. https://doi.org/10.19173/irrodl.v19i4.3601

Chapter 1 Appendices

Appendix A: Collaborative Syllabus Discussion Questions

Instructors can use a variety of questions designed to solicit student collaboration on the syllabus. These questions are inspired and derived from the existing literature on collaborative course design (e.g., Aiken et al., 2016; Murray, 2021). These questions include:

1. What do you want to learn in this course?
2. What kinds of activities will help you learn best?
3. What's your one big question? "I really want to know...."
4. How would you like to meet for office hours (Zoom or Face-to-Face)?
5. How can you best demonstrate your learning? (e.g., essays, quizzes, exams, other)

Appendix B: Examples of Students' Collaborative Responses

Group 1	Group 2
What would you like to learn? • Developing a social media presence for a brand/business. • Increasing engagement (what does it?) • Mastering algorithms! • Finer details of partnerships/sponsors • Harnessing humor *What helps you learn?* • Applied projects • Games • Group/Class discussions *Big Question:* • What are the three most important tools for creating a successful social media presence?	*What would you like to learn?* • Application of social media strategies. • What social media looks like in practice. *What helps you learn?* • Applying class content from learned strategies. *Big Question:* • We really want to know what role social media plays in a business setting.

Group 2	Group 3
What would you like to learn? • Create a cohesive brand and brand values that can be expressed on social media and follow trends accurately. *What helps you learn?* • In class discussion of real examples • Hands-on activities *Big Question:* • How to be successful on social media?	*What would you like to learn?* • Creating a professional social media account • Good and bad examples of PR and social media (and why) • Effective social media strategies that can be applied in the real world. • Effects of influencers. • How to measure success on social media. *What helps you learn?* • Real-world examples and applications • Projects/portfolio style work *Big Question:* • How can we use social media to be successful in our careers?

2. Art in Engineering as Open Educational Resources

Jean Hertzberg, PhD

Chapter Learning Objectives:

- Construct a course or module based on visual aesthetics in a nominally objective subject.
- Recognize how including visual aesthetics can improve diversity and inclusion.
- Produce an OER website combining student and instructor artwork and scientific documentation.
- Implement the Critical Response Process in peer critique of student work.

Chapter Overview

"Flow Visualization: The Art and Physics of Fluid Flow" is a 20-year-old technical elective in the Mechanical Engineering program at the University of Colorado Boulder. I developed the course to give both engineering and art students the opportunity to explore the interface between art and science, an interface that is open to everyone but which is often not valued in engineering education. In this course (abbreviated here as the Flow Vis course), students make aesthetic visualizations (photographic images or videos) that illustrate the physics of gasses and liquids. Students then write reports that describe the fluid physics and the methods of making the visualization in sufficient detail so that other students can duplicate the visualization. Students are instructed in optics, photography, specific flow visualization techniques, technical communication, and critique. What is not included is also important: students are not told to use specific techniques or study specific fluid physics. Instead, they are asked to be creative, play with fluids and photography, and let the art drive the science. They find their own aesthetic visions in the process.

This course exemplifies open pedagogy in that students make use of open educational resources (OER) and produce them. All student work is published on a high visibility and archival website, https://Flowvis.org, under a Creative Commons license. Together, the visualization and report make the knowledge students acquired during each formative assessment available on a global basis. Furthermore, all course materials, including syllabus, schedule, lecture notes and lecture video recordings, assignment details, and an OER textbook by the instructor (Hertzberg, 2024a) using student work as examples, are published on the same website. In this way, the instructor and students have co-created an OER.

Focused Questions:

1. What elements of your discipline are visually beautiful or powerful that could be used to inspire students' intrinsic motivation to engage with course content?
2. What benefits might students' disciplinary artwork offer beyond personal satisfaction and growth, particularly in raising awareness of important issues?

Rationale

Open pedagogy encompasses various practices that share common features, as noted by Clinton-Lisell (2021), including the emphasis on students producing innovative and valuable artifacts that extend beyond mere learning, often involving renewable assignments intended for public sharing and open licensing. The definitions of renewable assignments (Wiley & Hilton, 2018) and non-disposable assignments (NDAs) (Seraphin et al., 2019) overlap to a great extent. Wiley and Hilton (2018) outline four criteria for open pedagogy: (a) The student creates an artifact, (b) The artifact holds value beyond supporting the student's learning, (c) The artifact is made public, and (d) The artifact is openly licensed. These criteria are all met in the Flow Vis course, as discussed below. Additionally, Seraphin et al. (2019) provide further criteria, including revision, creativity, modification of objectives, cooperative critique, and innovation potential.

In contrast to typical 'hands-on' engineering courses where students follow specific lab procedures or work on proprietary client-driven problems, students in Flow Vis choose their study topics and methods. First, students are given an open-ended prompt to create a photograph or video of physical phenomena featuring gasses or liquids. In truth, students often begin with only a vague idea of what to do, perhaps inspired by a previous student's visualization or a strange YouTube video. For example, recently, students have been fascinated by "Elephant's Toothpaste," a startling eruption of foam from a mixture of hydrogen peroxide, potassium iodine, and soap (Rober, 2019).

They then assemble their apparatus out of their daily environment: kitchens, bathrooms, and the sky outside. Students also have access to university resources such as large flow facilities like flumes and wind tunnels, some research laboratories, various small fluids demonstrations, and photographic equipment. The nonlinearity of fluid flows practically guarantees they won't be able to replicate their inspiration exactly. Instead, students create a novel result that illustrates a phenomenon that may have escaped scientific scrutiny. Much of the science of fluid mechanics has been driven by military and industrial applications, limiting its scope. In contrast, student work motivated by aesthetics has often generated new knowledge.

Simply setting students free to explore satisfies two criteria for a non-disposable assignment: modification of objectives and chance innovation (Seraphin et al., 2019). Using such non-disposable assignments is rare in engineering education; instead, faculty jealously guard solutions to exams and homework sets in the hope of preventing plagiarism. Exceptions may be found in freshman and senior design courses, but public dissemination of project outcomes is still rare. In the Flow Vis course, the opposite approach is used. Students are expected to be inspired by and build upon previous students' work and contribute their work for the use of future students and the public.

The Flow Vis course heavily emphasizes renewable assignments, requiring students to complete six projects that feature an image or video created with artistic and intellectual control, along with a detailed report explaining the visualization process and the physics illustrated. This report is essential for ensuring the scientific usefulness of the work and is a reasonable expectation for all students. Additionally, this activity aligns with the concept of "building OERs with your students" (DeRosa & Jhangiani, 2017, para. 17), as students contribute bite-sized, stand-alone resources.

Collaborative learning, a key aspect of open pedagogy, is implemented in two ways in each course assessment. The first is an unusual modification of a traditional approach. Traditionally, engineering students are placed in teams to accomplish a project and collaborate to produce a single deliverable package. Each student's performance on the team may or may not be graded individually, and both approaches are problematic. For example, it is often difficult to identify a student's contribution to the project. In Flow Vis, students are placed in teams for mutual support but are expected to produce unique work. Since this differs significantly from their prior team experiences, the following team expectations and reasons for collaboration are explicitly outlined for students:

1. To allow students to attempt imaging more complex flow phenomena by distributing the work of developing a setup across the team, enabling the exploration of more challenging experiments.
2. To allow students to try more advanced imaging techniques by pooling photographic and fluid expertise and equipment within the team.
3. To encourage collaboration, allowing students to bounce ideas off one another, fostering creativity and idea generation.
4. To offer informal feedback from team members on each student's work.

5. To enable students to interact with peers from diverse backgrounds (Hertzberg, 2024b).

The second area where collaborative learning is implemented in the Flow Vis course is via formal peer critique using the Critical Response Process (Lerman, 2002). Students are trained in a highly supportive and constructive critique method. In this oral critique process, students present their work to small groups during class and get feedback.

In addition to the oral feedback, students review two peers' written reports using the "Rubric for Self and Peer Assessment," a check-plus style rubric (see Appendix A), and are then encouraged to revise and repost both their visualizations and reports. This satisfies two more criteria for open pedagogy: collaborative learning and opportunities for revision (Seraphin et al., 2019, p. 86). Importantly, participation in the critique is mandatory but does not impact the course grade, ensuring that critique remains a formative, learning-centered activity. Further details on the critique process, including roles and facilitation, are described in the 'Peer and Expert Critiques' section below.

Assessment Description

Students complete six assignments spread over the semester. These assignments have similar learning objectives and share a common formative assessment structure, including critique format and report rubric. The first assignment, 'Get Wet,' will be described in detail.

The learning objectives for the course comprise these common elements of each assignment's objectives:

1. Train your perception of fluid physics in the real world.
2. Employ aesthetics (art) as a valid method for exploring fluid physics.
3. Demonstrate the ability to communicate aesthetics and fluid physics to a wide audience.
4. Critique your peers using supportive but substantive techniques.
5. Demonstrate basic skills in scientific and artistic imaging: focus, exposure, and composition.
6. Design and analyze flow visualization experiments.

Of the six assignments, three are completed as individuals and three as team members. Early in the semester, students are surveyed using the CATME platform for their schedules, demographics, photography experience, and equipment. CATME algorithmically creates teams based on the instructor's parameters, such as similarity of schedules and dissimilarity of photography experience. 'Get Wet' is completed individually, as are two 'cloud' assignments that involve photographing atmospheric clouds throughout the semester. The other three assignments are done in teams, where students assist each other in creating visualizations, although each student is still responsible for a unique visualization and report.

Part A: The First Assignment 'Get Wet'

On the first day of class, students receive a list of initial assignments, including logistical tasks like reading the syllabus and joining the Slack workspace, along with two substantive assignments: 'Get Wet' and 'Clouds First.' The 'Get Wet' assignment focuses on recognizing the challenges of creating an accurate and aesthetically pleasing flow visualization. Students are encouraged to "get their feet wet" by capturing images or videos of fluids (air, water, gas, or liquid) that effectively demonstrate observed phenomena while also being visually appealing. They can use any familiar imaging technique—analog or digital, still or video, in black and white or color. Additional instructions guide students on publishing their work on Flowvis.org and submitting an archival version to Canvas, the university's learning management system. This assignment is due in the third week of the semester, and lectures during that period are designed to support completion. They cover flow visualization techniques, camera technologies, and image editing tutorials.

Part C: The Written Report for 'Get Wet' Assignment

The six visualization assignments are critiqued two days after the image/video is submitted online to both Flowvis.org and Canvas. Students are assigned to small 'critique pods' of 8 to 10. The pods meet simultaneously in Zoom breakout rooms during the regular class period. The students perform most of the critique and are very successful at addressing the aesthetic and photographic aspects of the work. Still, even the most advanced Mechanical Engineering student does not have the background to assess the wide range of fluid physics that students reveal in their work. Thus, an expert in fluid mechanics participates as well. The expert's role is to help the artist (the presenting student) describe the fluid physics in the visualization and provide keywords for the artist to use in researching the physics for the written report, due a week later. The experts are a mix of paid and volunteer research and science communication professionals drawn from university faculties and research laboratories. Every student's work is critiqued using the Critical Response Process (Lerman, 2002). A facilitator moderates a discussion between the artist and the responders (students in the audience). Students each take a turn as facilitators at least once over the course of the semester and thus gain experience with all three roles. The discussion is structured in five stages:

1. Artist presents the work. Students briefly describe their flow and photography setup.
2. Statements of meaning (usually positive). Responders are given the following prompts for this stage when the method is introduced:
   a. What does this image/video say about fluids? What is being shown?

b. What does this image/video say about aesthetics? Does it strike you with beauty, power, destruction, oddness, or other aesthetic?

c. What does this image/video say about the imaging technique? Does it impress you or inspire questions?

d. Are there other meanings in the image/video?

e. If making a positive comment, be honest and specific. What did you like and why? Do not just say, 'good job.'

3. Questions from the artist to the responders. The student presenting is expected to ask for specific feedback to guide further development of the work, such as:

a. What do you think of the way the image is cropped?

b. What about how color is presented in the image?

c. Did you notice where the light pole is edited out?

Students are told "Don't ask just 'what do you think'; that's too vague. You will get more useful answers if your question is focused."

4. Neutral questions (questions without embedded opinions) from the responders to the artist. This stage is the most difficult for responders, sometimes requiring the facilitator to help by rephrasing the question. Students are told, "It is tough to ask a question without embedding an opinion. It will take practice. For example, instead of 'it's kind of dark' or 'why is it so dark at the bottom?' ask, 'what do you think about the balance of light and dark areas?' Be sure to ask about the fluid physics: 'why does it look like that?'"

5. Permissioned opinions. Responders name the topic of their opinion and then ask the artist for permission to state it. For example, 'I have an opinion about the depth of field and the focus. Do you want to hear it?' The artist can answer yes or no. If they already know that the focus was bad and what to do, they can say 'no thanks.' This stage allows responders to voice opinions that they couldn't fit into other stages of the critique while still giving the artist a measure of control.

The Critical Response Process defuses the natural defensive reaction to criticism of one's work and makes it easy for audience members to provide truly constructive comments. Engineering students are now more willing to offer remarks in class. In exit surveys, some students objected to the method as being overly structured, while others appreciated the method, noting its utility in other contexts.

Get Wet Part C: The Written Report

Students document their work for each major assignment in a written report, which is added to their post on Flowvis.org and submitted on Canvas two weeks after the oral critiques. They describe their artistic approach and as much of the fluid physics as they can. All students are also expected to explain their setups in sufficient detail so that someone else could recreate the experiment. This level of documentation is normal for engineering students while novel for art students. The importance of such documentation for artists is emphasized, noting that it will improve their control over their tools, techniques, and work.

The course grade uses a labor-based contract grading ("Contract Grading," 2023) approach, where students are expected to complete their assignments at a level appropriate to their backgrounds, and their course grade is based on completing the work. In support of this approach, I developed the "Rubric for Self and Peer Assessment" for assessing student work based on four categories: photographic technique, whether the artistic intent was achieved, whether a fluid phenomenon was made visible, and whether there was appropriate content in the written report. Students use the "Rubric for Self and Peer Assessment" primarily for self-assessment of the written report and secondarily for peer critique of the reports. Each student is randomly assigned to give peer critiques of two written reports for each of the six major assignments using this rubric; this is easily implemented in Canvas.

Debrief

One of the key benefits of renewable assignments is their positive impact on student motivation (Abri & Dabbagh, 2019; Baran & AlZoubi, 2020; Stancil, 2020). Engineering students are often motivated by the points awarded for completing assignments and exams. However, this type of grading is deliberately avoided in the Flow Vis course. Instead, contract grading ("Contract Grading," 2023) and ungrading statements (Blackwelder et al., 2020) are used to assess course performance, aiming to promote intrinsic motivation. The agency and empowerment fostered by publication are expected to contribute to this goal (Seraphin et al., 2019). Early in the semester, when surveyed about their motivations, students primarily cited creative freedom and aesthetics rather than publication. The impact of the renewable assignment on motivation later in the semester, after students have engaged with publication, is still unknown. A possible synergy between creating an artifact with scientific and artistic value and its subsequent publication may further enhance motivation. To explore this, a survey is being designed (Scribner et al., 2021).

Student work is reused and remixed locally in the course by students in subsequent semesters. In both conceiving the visualization and writing the report, students use a variety of freely available educational resources, including student work from previous semesters as published on Flowvis.org, as well as other OER such as Wikipedia and YouTube. For example, a student exploring soap films may read a previous student's description of their apparatus and procedure before attempting their own, then turn to a professional soap film artist's blog about best practices for lighting. Students are expected to cite all published resources, including copyrighted material from relevant technical literature such as textbooks and professional journals.

In the Flow Visualization course, open licensing has allowed assignments to meet the criteria for renewable assignments, as proposed by Wiley and Hilton (2018). Since 2003, student work has been published on the course website, initially under traditional copyright, and later, in 2016, a shift to Creative Commons licensing was considered. A survey at that time revealed most students favored a more open approach, though 27% expressed concerns about commercial uses and preferred to prevent corporations from profiting from their work. This led to the adoption of a restrictive license (Attribution-NonCommercial-NoDerivatives) to balance student concerns with copyright protections. Interestingly, many students were unaware of the complexities of licensing. Despite the requirement for student work to be published, no alumni (out of 676 surveyed) raised concerns about licensing. However, one student with a background in online security requested their name be removed from their work.

All content on the Flow Vis website is licensed as CC-BY (Attribution Only), aligning with open remixing practices. However, students retain copyright over the highest resolution versions of their images, which are not published on the website. Through a formal Copyright Use Agreement developed with university legal counsel (see Appendix B), students consent to allow academic use of these original images. This agreement has enabled the inclusion of students' images in textbooks, journal articles, and promotional material for the University of Colorado.

In the Fall of 2024, a survey assessed student familiarity with Creative Commons licenses. While 35% had never heard of Creative Commons and only one student understood license differences, after discussion, 75% supported CC-BY, believing "knowledge should never be restricted," and 25% favored CC-BY-SA, emphasizing sharing of derivative works.

Appraisal

Student work submitted in response to the first assignment often exceeds expectations, even though some students have no prior fluid mechanics or imaging background and have yet to receive extensive instruction in these areas. This demonstrates the effectiveness of the course's approach in fostering learning and engagement. For example, Figure 1 illustrates the graceful movement of low-speed fluid flows, specifically showing laminar flow as a falling droplet of cream penetrates the water and then rises due to the Rayleigh-Taylor instability. This phenomenon occurs because unwhipped cream is less dense than water due to its fat content (Rayleigh–Taylor Instability, 2023). The ability of students to create such detailed and accurate depictions despite limited prior knowledge underscores the success of the course's focus on accessibility and experiential learning.

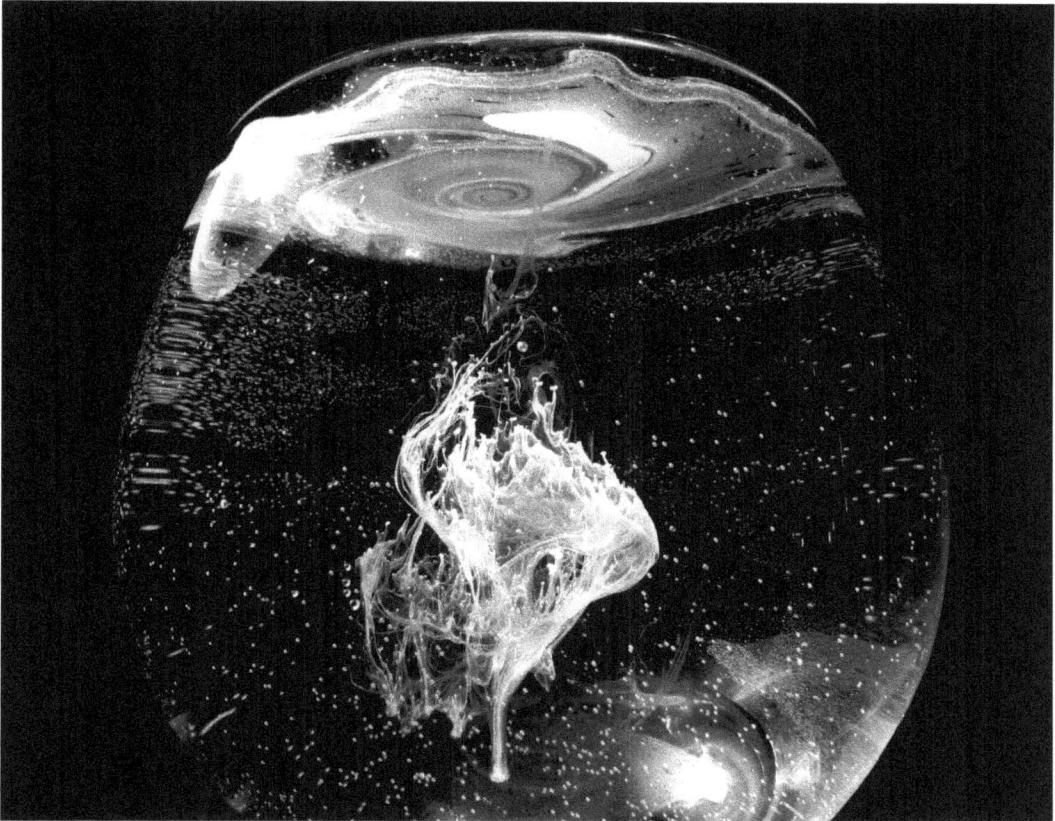

Figure 1: An Example of The Flow Visualization Aesthetic of Beauty. Whipping cream dropped into a glass of water returns to the top surface in the form of tiny columns. By Janelle Montoya, for the Get Wet assignment Fall 2015.

The artist was Janelle Montoya, an undergraduate mechanical engineering student who had completed a course in fluid mechanics but had no background in imaging. In her report, provided in Appendix C, she describes how the cream illustrates the beauty of the swirling flow and the difficulty of avoiding reflections. She concludes that she satisfied her intent with the accuracy of the image.

Figure 2 presents a striking aesthetic, demonstrating fluid phenomena's surprising and often paradoxical nature. Although humans intuitively understand fluid flows, the oddness of certain fluid behaviors can still be surprising. For example, Figure 2 contrasts the upraised thumb, symbolizing a positive, joyful reaction, with our instinctual withdrawal from flames, creating an aesthetic of curiosity and contradiction. This represents the exploration of fluid phenomena from a more creative perspective.

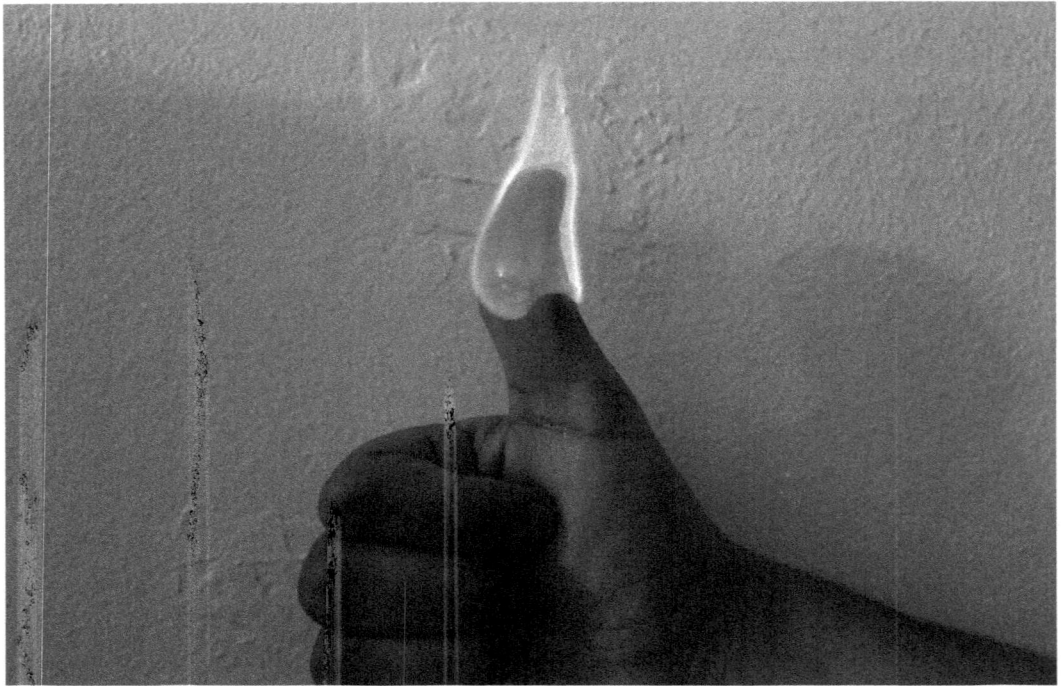

Figure 2: An Example of The Aesthetic of Oddness. Peppermint schnapps burns briefly by Kevin Oh.

However, despite this creative visual approach, Kevin Oh, a Mechanical Engineering undergraduate, must fully integrate this analysis into his report. While the visual work is compelling, the lack of deeper analysis in the written component suggests an area for growth in balancing aesthetic exploration with scientific reasoning. This gap highlights an opportunity for future course improvements in guiding students to connect their creative work with more rigorous analysis.

Open pedagogy is most successful when student work reaches a larger community, and the Flow Vis course exemplifies this through its global audience. The course website, https://FlowVis.org, attracts visitors who are either drawn by the aesthetics of the visualizations or are searching for examples of specific fluid phenomena. Beginning in 2007, the website was the top result on Google for "flow visualization," maintaining this status for many years before being overtaken by SEO-driven sites like Wikipedia and NASA. The website is still in the top few results and continues to draw a steady stream of traffic, with approximately 10,000 annual visitors since 2018, as shown in Figure 3. In the most recent year (October 2023–September 2024), 30% of the 27,543 views came from non-English-speaking countries, spanning 130 nations. This broad international engagement highlights the reach and success of the course's open pedagogy approach in promoting global knowledge sharing. Details are provided in Appendix D.

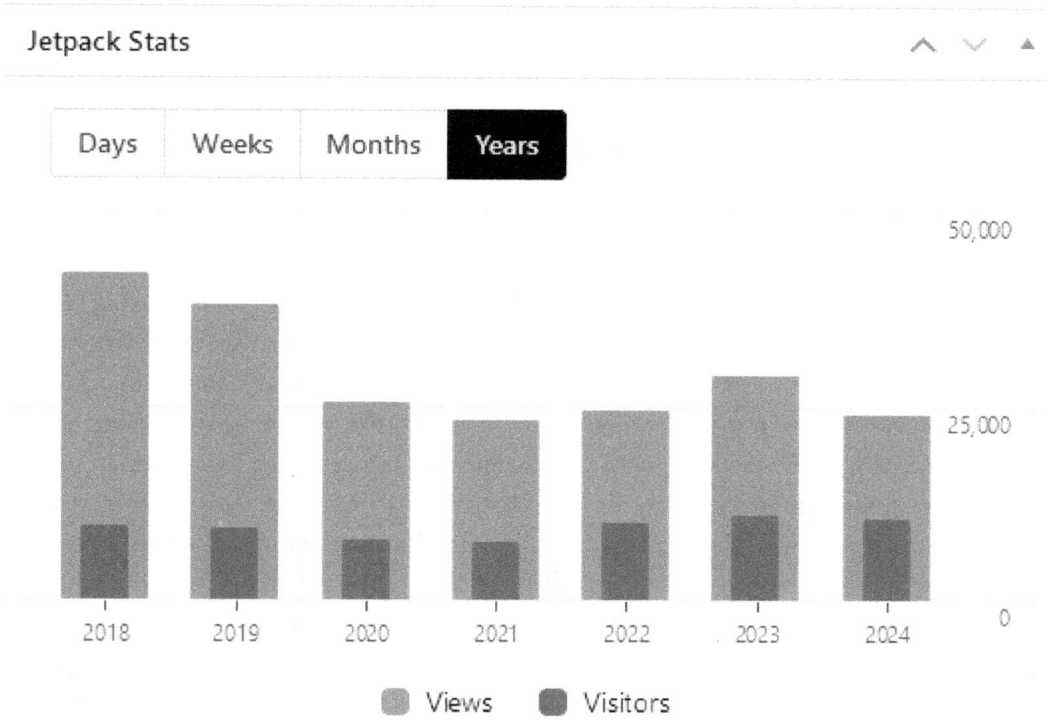

Figure 3: Site Statistics for https://Flowvis.org taken as a Screenshot on 12/6/2024

Seraphin et al. (2019) propose a framework for evaluating NDAs based on time, space, and gravity. Flow Visualization assignments excel in these areas. The website has existed for 20 years, with plans for future growth, demonstrating its strong performance on the time scale. On the space scale, the site ranks highly and is used globally. In terms of gravity—defined as the "extent of value/impact" (Seraphin et al., 2019)—the course has had a transformative effect on students, expanding their perception and motivating them to analyze fluid physics and appreciate its aesthetics (Goodman, 2015; Goodman et al., 2018; Pugh, 2011). The impact extends beyond students, as fluid mechanics educators have adapted the course for use at 12 universities, further enhancing the gravity of the Flow Vis NDAs.

The Flow Vis course and website have successfully reached a global audience, with a significant percentage of visitors from non-English-speaking countries. However, there is potential to further amplify the social justice aspects of the course by enhancing its appeal to diverse audiences. One possible improvement is integrating an automatic language translation service to make the content more accessible to non-English speakers. Evaluating the effectiveness of this initiative through website usage statistics could provide valuable insights into its impact on engagement and inclusivity, further strengthening the course's commitment to accessibility and global participation.

Beyond simple language accessibility, DeRosa and Jhangiani (2017) argue that open pedagogy reduces costs and democratizes knowledge creation, making it accessible to all rather than an elite domain. In the Flow Visualization course, this principle is reflected in the accessibility of course content and the expectation that engineering students engage in artistic practices while art students explore engineering concepts. Inclusivity is further enhanced through assignments focusing on everyday physics, which can be easily observed and understood with minimal equipment and basic mathematics. This approach is particularly crucial for scientific topics, where barriers to participation can be significant. Fluid mechanics, often perceived as a challenging subject by engineering students and the general public, is made more approachable; the complexity lies primarily in mathematics, not the underlying physics.

Conducting critique sessions remotely offers several benefits that enhance accessibility and efficiency. First, it ensures equitable participation for fully remote students when the course is taught in a hybrid mode, leveling the playing field by having all students engage remotely. Second, it alleviates the need to schedule conference rooms for in-person participants, addressing a significant limitation on class size. Since each student's work is critiqued in 10–15-minute intervals, the need for multiple simultaneous critique sessions across several class periods can be met more easily through remote sessions. This also eliminates the challenge of securing conference rooms with the appropriate videoconferencing technology. Finally, the remote format facilitates participation by distant fluid mechanics experts, allowing for greater expertise and variety in feedback. Overall, the shift to remote critique sessions has improved the logistics and inclusivity of the course, benefiting both students and external contributors.

The structure of the Flow Vis course can be readily applied to other science, technology, engineering, art, and math (STEAM) courses. Students can be invited to create aesthetic representations illustrating the fundamental concepts, write about them, and publish the results with an open license. An example of application in a different STEAM topic is a course in engineering design: the Aesthetics of Design course at the University of Colorado.

Extending this course structure to disciplines outside of STEAM is straightforward as long as aesthetics relevant to the discipline can be imagined. Having an aesthetic component ensures endless variations in student work, with each example providing a unique perspective on the topic, thus allowing the published resource to grow in value with each successive semester's offering. Even without an aesthetic component, some of the tools described here will be useful for other pedagogies, such as the Critical Response Process for peer critique or an ongoing blog site for the publication of student work.

Summary

In closing, the Flow Visualization course exemplifies open pedagogy in numerous ways, allowing students to blend aesthetics with scientific inquiry as they navigate the intersection of art and science. The high visibility of their work on a well-established, globally-recognized archival website enhances its reach over time and space, as outlined in Seraphin et al.'s (2019) framework. Furthermore, the course has significantly impacted students and faculty, contributing to its overall gravity within this framework. Ultimately, the Flow Vis course highlights the utility and value of open pedagogy in engineering education, underscoring the importance of empowering students to unleash their creativity.

References

Abri, M. H. A., & Dabbagh, N. (2019). Testing the intervention of OER renewable assignments in a college course. *Open Praxis*, *11*(2), 195-209. https://doi.org/10.5944/open-praxis.11.2.916

Baran, E., & AlZoubi, D. (2020). Affordances, challenges, and impact of open pedagogy: Examining students' voices. *Distance Education*, *41*(2), 230–244. https://doi.org/10.1080/01587919.2020.1757409

Blackwelder, A., Blum, S. D., Chiaravalli, A., Chu G., Davidson, C., Gibbs, L., Katopodis, C., Kirr, J., Kohn, A., Riesbeck, C., Sackstein, S., Schultz-Bergin, M., Sorensen-Unruh, C., Stommel, J. & Warner, J. (2020). Ungrading: Why rating students undermines learning. In S. D. Blum, (Ed.), *How to ungrade* (pp. 35-36). West Virginia University Press.

Clinton-Lisell, V. (2021). Open pedagogy: A systematic review of empirical findings. *Journal of Learning for Development*, *8*(2), 255–268. https://doi.org/10.56059/jl4d.v8i2.511

Contract grading. (2023, January 5). In *Wikipedia*. https://en.wikipedia.org/w/index.php?title=Contract_grading&oldid=1131731023

DeRosa, R., & Jhangiani, R. S. (2017). *Open pedagogy: A guide to making open textbooks with students*. https://press.rebus.community/makingopentextbookswithstudents/chapter/open-pedagogy/

Goodman, K. (2015). *The transformative experience in engineering education* [Doctoral dissertation, University of Colorado]. The ATLAS Institute repository. https://www.colorado.edu/atlas/sites/default/files/attached-files/the_transformative_experience_in_engineering_eduaction.pdf

Goodman, K., Hertzberg, J., & Finkelstein, N. (2018). Surely you must be joking, Mr. Twain! Re-engaging science students through visual aesthetics. *Leonardo*, *53*(3), 311–315. https://doi.org/10.1162/LEON_a_01604

Hertzberg, J. (2024a). *The flow visualization guidebook*. https://www.flowvis.org/Flow%20Vis%20Guide/introduction-to-the-guidebook/

Hertzberg, J. (2024b). *Team expectations*. https://flowvis.org/media/course/TeamExpectations.pdf

Lerman, L. (2002). *Critical response process: A method for getting useful feedback on anything you make, from dance to dessert*. Liz Lerman Dance Exchange.

Pugh, K. J. (2011). Transformative experience: An integrative construct in the spirit of Deweyan pragmatism. *Educational Psychologist*, 46(2), 107–121. https://doi.org/10.1080/00461520.2011.558817

Rayleigh–Taylor instability. (2023). *Wikipedia*. https://en.wikipedia.org/w/index.php?title=Rayleigh%E2%80%93Taylor_instability&oldid=1176070139

Rober, M. (Director). (2019, August 29). *World's largest elephant toothpaste experiment* [Video recording]. https://www.youtube.com/watch?v=Kou7ur5xt_4

Scribner, H., Goodman, K., & Hertzberg, J. (2021, June 9). *The influence of aesthetics on engineering learning* [Presentation/Workshop]. ASEE Rocky Mountain Section Unconference 2021, Online. http://www.uwyo.edu/asee/rms/details.html

Seraphin, S. B., Grizzell, J. A., Kerr-German, A., Perkins, M. A., Grzanka, P. R., & Hardin, E. E. (2019). A conceptual framework for non-disposable assignments: Inspiring implementation, innovation, and research. *Psychology Learning & Teaching*, 18(1), 84-97. https://doi.org/10.1177/1475725718811711

Stancil, S. K. (2020). *Exploring working graduate students' experiences with reusable assignments* [Doctoral dissertation, North Carolina State University]. Proquest. https://www.proquest.com/docview/2400696925/abstract/89347948CE084B4CPQ/1

Wiley, D., & Hilton III, J. L. (2018). Defining OER-enabled pedagogy. *The International Review of Research in Open and Distributed Learning*, 19(4), 133-147. https://doi.org/10.19173/irrodl.v19i4.3601

Media Attributions

Chapter 2 Appendices

Appendix A: Rubric for Self and Peer Assessment

Scale:

- +, ! = excellent
- √ = meets expectations; good.
- ~ = Ok, could be better.
- X = needs work.
- NA = not applicable

Art	Your assessment	Comments
Intent was realized		
Effective		
Impact		
Interesting		
Beautiful		
Dramatic		
Feel/texture		
No distracting elements		
Framing/cropping enhances image		

Flow	Your assessment	Comments
Clearly illustrates phenomena		
Flow is understandable		
Physics revealed		
Details visible		
Flow is reproducible		
Flow is controlled		
Creative flow or technique		
Publishable quality		

Photographic/video technique	Your assessment	Comments
Exposure: highlights detailed		
Exposure: shadows detailed		

Photographic/video technique	Your assessment	Comments
Full contrast range		
Focus		
Depth of field		
Time resolved		
Spatially resolved		
Photoshop/ post-processing enhances intent		
Photoshop/ post-processing does not decrease important information		

Report	Characteristics	Your assessment	Comments
Collaborators acknowledged			
Describes intent	Artistic		
	Scientific		
Describes fluid phenomena			
Estimates appropriate scales	Reynolds number etc.		
Calculation of time resolution etc.	How far did flow move during exposure?		
References:	Web level		
	Refereed journal level		
Clearly written			
Information is organized			
Good spelling and grammar			
Professional language (publishable)			
Provides information needed for reproducing flow	Fluid data, flow rates		
	geometry		
	timing		
Provides information needed for reproducing vis technique	Method		
	dilution		
	injection speed		
	settings		
Lighting type	(strobe/tungsten, watts, number)		
	light position, distance		
Provides information for reproducing image	Camera type and model		
	Camera-subject distance		

Report	Characteristics	Your assessment	Comments
	Field of view		
	Focal length		
	aperture		
	shutter speed		
	Frame rate, playback rate		
	ISO setting		
	# pixels (width X ht)		
	Editing and post-processing techniques		
	"before" editing image is included		

Appendix B: Copyright Agreement

THIS COPYRIGHT AGREEMENT (hereinafter "Agreement") is between Professor Jean Hertzberg (hereinafter Professor) and _____ (hereinafter "Student").

WHEREAS, Student has or will participate in the Course "Flow Visualization" (hereinafter "Course") at the University of Colorado, the purpose of which is to provide Student with experience applying skills and knowledge in the field of physics and art of visualizing and photographic recording of fluid flows; and

WHEREAS, the professor of this class Jean Hertzberg (hereinafter "Professor"), desire to use materials developed by the Student (hereinafter "Creative Work") for instructional purposes or for use in Professor's scholarly publication and outreach activities; and

WHEREAS, Student is willing to allow such use of his/her Creative Work;

NOW THEREFORE, in consideration of University granting Student permission to work on the Project, and in consideration of the mutual promises described herein, the parties hereto agree as follows:

1. **Use.**

    A. Student hereby grants Professor the right to use the Creative Work, including any copyrights or other intellectual property rights that may apply to such Creative Work, solely for the following purposes:

        1. For Professor's personal instructional purposes at the University of Colorado;

        2. For recruitment and publicity for the University of Colorado;

        3. For use in Professor's non-commercial scholarly publication(s) with appropriate citation of the Creative Work accorded to the Student as described in Section 2.

B. Professor hereby agrees not to use the Creative Work for any other purpose than specifically described herein without prior written permission.

2. **Public Acknowledgment.**

Professor agrees to appropriately acknowledge the Student's Creative Work in any publication or instructional materials developed by Professor.

IN WITNESS WHEREOF the parties have executed this Agreement as of the date first below written.

Professor

- Printed Name:
- Date:
- Signature:

Student

- Printed Name:
- Date:
- Signature:

Appendix C: Student Work Example

"Get Wet Report"

Flow Visualization by Janelle Montoya, Sept. 25, 2015

Note: This appendix is formatted according to the student's assignment requirements.

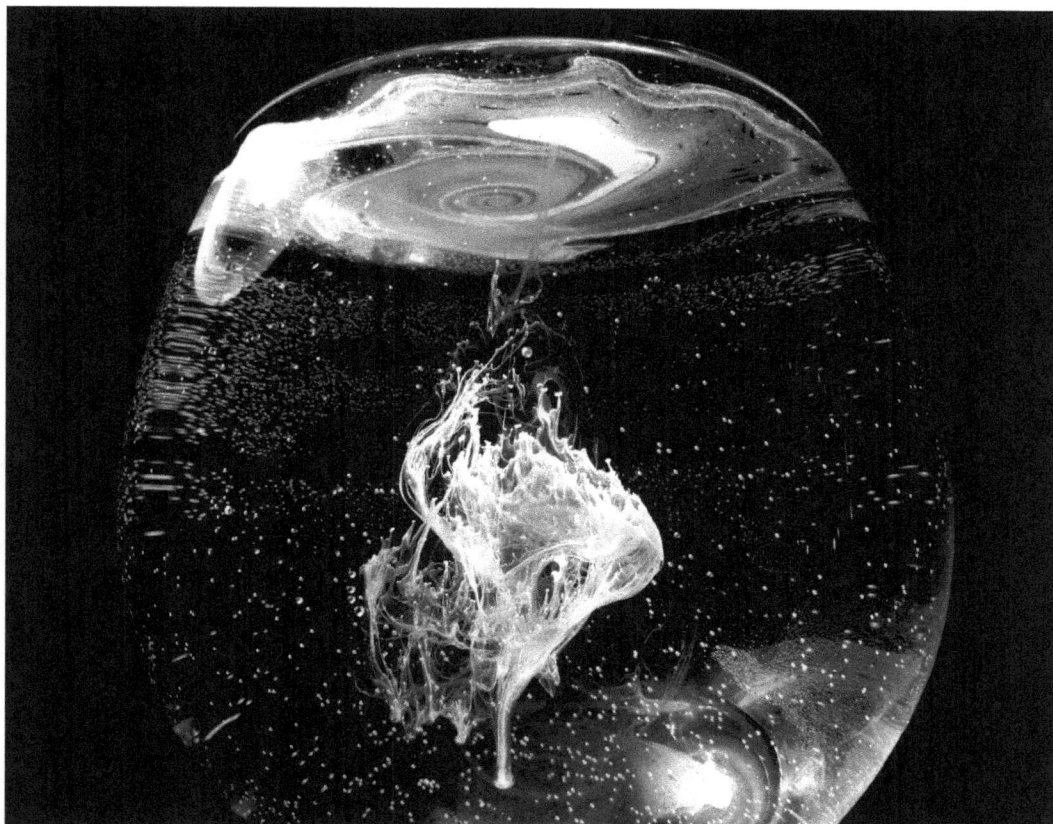

Figure 1: Final "Get Wet" Image: Cream Castle

1 Purpose

The purpose of this visualization was to capture the nature of whipping cream and the fluid dynamics that result from the billowing plumes that arise when it is dropped into a pool of water. The phenomena was initially observed by trying the experiment with cold whipping cream in warm water, which yielded interesting tower-like structures that would form out of a single drop. The shot was captured thanks to the help of my roommate, Allyssa, who dropped the cream into the water.

2 Apparatus

The apparatus used in the image was a wine glass filled with warm water at the highest temperature from the tap in my apartment, which falls in the range of 85°to 90°Fahrenheit. Bubbles that were going to appear at the foreground of the image were scraped from the inside of the glass, so as not to cause any focusing on the bubbles that would appear in front of the cream that would be dropped into the water. Then, a liquid dropper was filled with cold (kept in the refrigerator at 40°F) Grade A ultra-pasteurized whipping cream, which contains approximately 35% fat. The water was allowed approximately 1 minute of settling time before the dropper was held about an inch above the surface and a single drop was released. The visualization occurs approximately 20-25 seconds after the cream has been dropped and has had time to interact with the warm water. A diagram of the setup can be seen below.

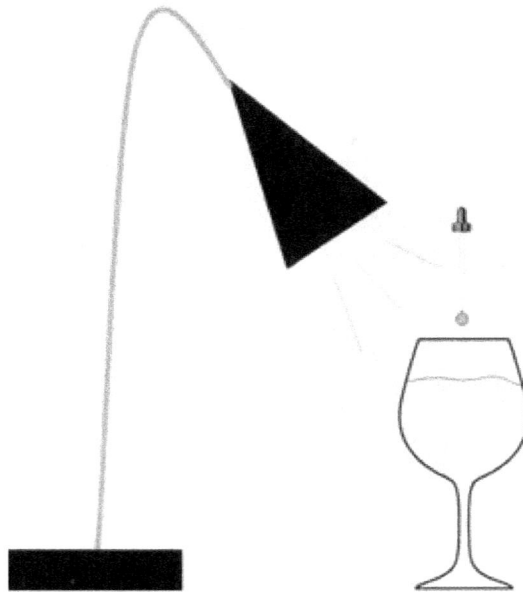

Figure 2: Image of Visualization Set Up

Visualization Set Up

The fluid phenomenon occurring in the image is largely due to positive buoyancy, meaning that the entering fluid tends to rise. The result of the cream rising in the warm water is a visualized "plume" which is a column of one fluid rising through another, and is directly driven by buoyancy. In Turner (1962), the author discusses the nature of this plume and how the cap of the flow moves at a slower rate than the column producing it, approximately 0.6 times the mean velocity of the columnar stream. This is significant for understanding why the cream accumulates at the top of each of the columns present in the flow, which can be attributed to its velocity in this case.

This positive buoyancy that is occurring between the liquids can also be attributed to several other fluid properties that were present in this setup. The first of these properties is density, which is different between the two fluids used. A general characteristic of the whipping cream is that it contains a significant amount of fat in it, which tends to rise. In most cases of milk preparation, this fat is "skimmed" from the top of a cream, hence the term "skimmed milk". This image is a direct account of this fat rising to the top of the wine glass and accumulating in an aesthetically pleasing spiral form. Ihara et al. (2010) discusses the aggregation of more fat globules with increasing temperature as well, meaning that more fat builds up at warmer temperatures, thus increasing the buoyancy effects prevalent in the fluid. The fluid properties for water and whipping cream are listed in Table 1 below.

Table 1: *Fluid Properties of Water and Cream*

	Water	Heavy Cream
Density (kg/m³)	1000	994

Aside from simply having different densities at room temperature, the fact that the water was relatively hot also seems to increase the forcing effect of the fluid flow. These thermal forcing effects caused the reaction in the cream to happen a lot quicker than it would have in cold water. Later, the same experiment was attempted with cold water, which actually yielded less dramatic results (relatively slow movement and less columnar structures) since the similar temperatures did not cause any rapid forcing to occur in the cream. These reactions are due to the dependence of density on temperature. It was found that density does, in fact, change the flow scenario since the particles in the warmer liquid will move farther apart from each other and at a more rapid rate, as discussed by Plaza (2005).

The Reynolds number is a quantity of interest in this flow, to further understand the flow pattern at hand. The calculation for the Reynolds number is shown below, where the velocity of the flow was calculated based on the time a previous image of the flow was taken. To do this, the distance of the flow from the bottom of the 4.5″ tall wine glass was compared to an average of where the flow appears in the final shot, which occurs 19 seconds later. This calculation for velocity in the y-direction is also shown below:

$$v_y = \frac{\delta x}{t}$$
$$= \frac{0.0134m}{19s}$$
$$= 0.00070m/s$$
$$Re = \frac{\rho v L}{\mu}$$
$$= \frac{(994kg/m^3)(0.0007m/s)(0.0021m)}{(0.00289pa*s)}$$
$$= 0.51$$

1 Visualization Techniques

The visualization technique used is known as a seeded boundary, meaning the milky liquid is the seeding fluid, and the transparent water does not scatter or absorb any light which makes the seeding fluid more apparent. This causes a clear boundary to be visible, especially against the dark background that was utilized for this image.

The lighting used was a spotlight lamp with a 4.5 Watt LED, which produces 200 lumens. The equivalent warmth for this light is 2700 Kelvin, which gives off a bright and relatively warm color. The lamp was placed with the mouth shining onto the top of the glass at a 45° angle from the vertical, and about 4 inches above the top of the glass as was shown previously in the diagram of the setup. The lamp can be seen in the upper left corner of the original image for reference in a later section. This was the only light source in the room, and all other lights in the surrounding area were turned off.

2 Photographic Techniques

The setup was approximately 6 inches away from the camera lens, while the focal length was 4.3 inches. The digital camera that was used to perform this visualization is a Canon Power-Shot SX520 HS, with a focal length of 4.3-180.6mm, aperture 1:3.4-6.0. The settings used to capture the image are as follows:

- Shutter speed 1/60
- f/5.6
- ISO 800

The original image size was 4608 x 3456 pixels, while the final was 4320 x 3456 pixels. GIMP was used as the choice of image editing software, where post processing was performed to darken the black background behind the flow, and enhance the whites in the cream. This was achieved using the Curves feature by creating an "S" shaped curve. Also, the background of the original image has a piece of white paper as well as a visible spotlight that was edited out with the Paint tool by coloring over those features with black paint. Layers were also utilized to mirror the upper right corner of the wine glass onto the upper left side to eliminate the washed out corner from the bright LED light that was incident on that corner. Some cleaning up was done using the Dodge/Burn tool, which selectively brightens or darkens the area onto which the tool is applied, to cleanly blend this addition into the image. The original image is displayed below.

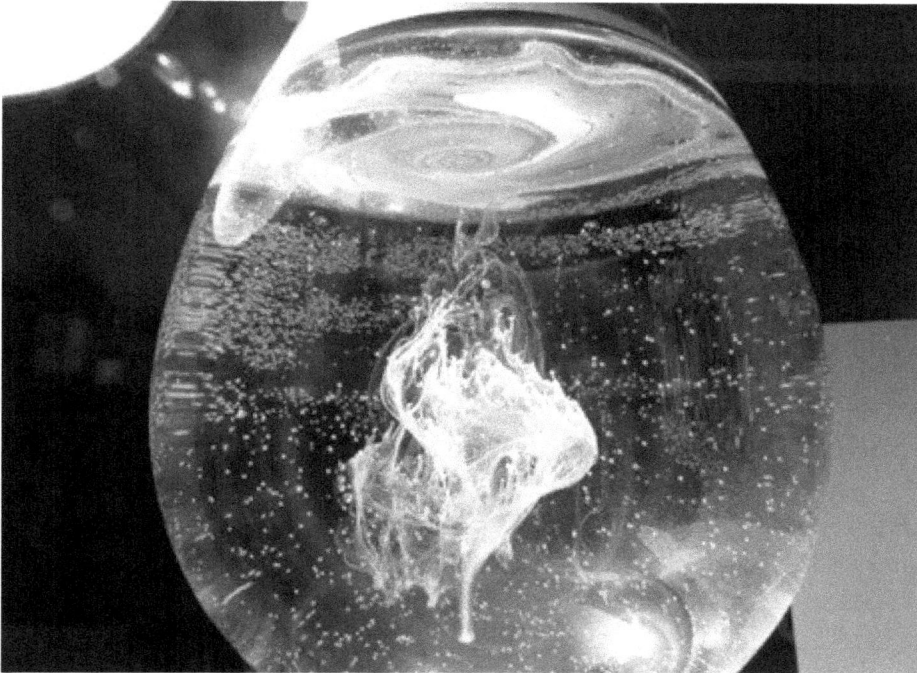

Figure 3: Original "Get Wet" Image: Cream Castle

3 Image Thoughts

This image reveals the beauty of fluid physics in a very clear way. With a very simple combination of fluids, an aesthetically pleasing image is realized. I like the focus on the fluid phenomena that is happening, as well as the swirl occurring at the top of the image due to the accumulation of the fat in the cream. I also think that the bubbles add a nice touch to the feeling of the fluid being enclosed in the wine glass in an otherwise dark place. In the future I might attempt to dilute the lighting so as not to produce such a strong reflection in the glass. I attempted to edit the reflections out of the image, but it proved too difficult to achieve with my level of image editing capabilities. With that being said, I believe that I realized my intent with this image, by capturing the suspended milk in water very clearly and without altering any of the information associated with the fluid flow that is occurring. If I were to develop this idea further, I would choose to observe creams of different fat contents, since heavier creams might tend to produce larger positive buoyancy reactions and perhaps larger plumes. Another development could involve changing the temperature of the water and observing where the threshold of this thermal forcing truly occurs.

References

Ihara, J. et al. (2010). Influence of whipping temperature on the whipping properties and rheological characteristics of whipped cream. *Journal of Dairy Science, 93*(7). 2887-2895. https://doi.org/10.3168/jds.2009-3012

Plaza, R. J. (2006). Sink or swim: The effects of temperature on liquid density and buoyancy. https://csef.usc.edu/History/2006/Projects/J1532.pdf

Turner, S. J. (1962). The 'starting plume' in neutral surroundings. Journal of *Fluid Mechanics, 13*(3), 356-368. https://doi.org/10.1017/S0022112062000762

Appendix D: Website View Statistics

Detail of https://Flowvis.org website views by country for October 2023 through September 2024, downloaded from Jetpack site statistics. English-speaking countries are highlighted.

Index	Country	Views	Index	Country	Views
1	**United States**	17460	81	Paraguay	6
2	**India**	1153	82	Georgia	5
3	**Australia**	742	83	Panama	5
4	**Canada**	731	84	Uruguay	5
5	Taiwan	688	85	Lebanon	4
6	**United Kingdom**	635	86	**Kenya**	4
7	Germany	524	87	Honduras	4
8	China	436	88	Azerbaijan	4
9	France	380	89	Latvia	4
10	South Korea	346	90	Bolivia	4
11	Brazil	281	91	Mongolia	3
12	Netherlands	244	92	Cyprus	3
13	**Philippines**	202	93	Zambia	3
14	Japan	189	94	**Malta**	3
15	Italy	187	95	Uzbekistan	3
16	Türkiye	155	96	Cambodia	3
17	Spain	152	97	Oman	2
18	Hong Kong SAR China	148	98	Bosnia & Herzegovina	2
19	Russia	136	99	Rwanda	2
20	**Singapore**	135	100	American Samoa	2
21	Indonesia	128	101	Macao SAR China	2
22	Mexico	126	102	Belarus	2

Index	Country	Views	Index	Country	Views
23	Belgium	114	103	Dominican Republic	2
24	Greece	109	104	**Ghana**	2
25	Poland	105	105	Guam	2
26	Israel	99	106	Guatemala	2
27	Thailand	92	107	**Trinidad & Tobago**	2
28	Denmark	88	108	Kosovo	2
29	Chile	80	109	St. Vincent & Grenadines	1
30	Sweden	73	110	Botswana	1
31	Switzerland	72	111	New Caledonia	1
32	Saudi Arabia	64	112	**Belize**	1
33	Finland	64	113	Montenegro	1
34	Nepal	63	114	Tanzania	1
35	Slovenia	61	115	Ethiopia	1
36	**South Africa**	59	116	Guernsey	1
37	Vietnam	56	117	**Jamaica**	1
38	Malaysia	56	118	**Bermuda**	1
39	Austria	56	119	Côte d'Ivoire	1
40	**New Zealand**	53	120	Cuba	1
41	Bulgaria	48	121	Libya	1
42	**Pakistan**	48	122	Zimbabwe	1
43	Czechia	43	123	**Barbados**	1
44	United Arab Emirates	43	124	Fiji	1
45	Norway	42	125	North Macedonia	1
46	Ukraine	40	126	Brunei	1
47	Bangladesh	39	127	Luxembourg	1
48	**Ireland**	38	128	El Salvador	1
49	Argentina	34	129	Albania	1
50	Colombia	33	130	Gibraltar	1
51	Romania	32	131	Eswatini	1
52	Egypt	32	132	Senegal	1
53	Slovakia	32	133	Namibia	1
54	Estonia	29	134	Mayotte	1
55	Portugal	26	135	Unknown Region	1
56	Tunisia	26		Total	27543
57	Iraq	24		English speaking	19621
58	Hungary	24			71%

Index	Country	Views	Index	Country	Views
59	Peru	23			
60	**Nigeria**	21			
61	Sri Lanka	19			
62	Puerto Rico	18			
63	Qatar	15			
64	Bahrain	13			
65	Uganda	13			
66	Armenia	13			
67	Croatia	11			
68	Algeria	11			
69	Venezuela	11			
70	Ecuador	11			
71	Jordan	10			
72	Iceland	9			
73	Serbia	8			
74	Madagascar	8			
75	Kuwait	7			
76	Morocco	7			
77	European Union	7			
78	Costa Rica	7			
79	Lithuania	6			
80	Myanmar (Burma)	6			

3. Scientific Research for the Non-Science Student: A Collaborative Observational Research Journey for a Concentrated Course or Stand-Alone Unit

Amanda Lohiser, PhD

Chapter Learning Objectives:

- To contextualize the scientific process as useful to non-science students as an avenue for critical and creative thinking.
- To explain in detail the guided observational research project process using one accelerated course as an example.
- To explore the application avenues for this project in other courses, fields of study, and teaching modalities.

Chapter Overview

How does one teach scientific research in an experiential way to students with no previous experience with or knowledge of the scientific process? When teaching undergraduate research methods-based courses that culminated with a research paper assessment, I noticed that students expressed trepidation at the scope of the assignment, with many indicating that they had not done anything like this before; in fact, many students had not yet experienced reading scholarly journal articles, writing citations in the proper format, or knowing when, how, and why to cite academic sources.

My answer to these questions in previous years was a great deal of one-on-one attention to individual students as these questions became apparent. My answer now is the assessment detailed in this chapter—an instructor-assisted document that guides students through the research process. The guide, titled *Research Projects for Beginners: A Guided Journey*, helps establish the answers to many "beginner" questions, enabling instructor-to-student dialogue to be more focused on developing ideas rather than directly teaching academic writing style and the basics of scientific research steps. Thus, the instructor-assisted guide document, explored in this chapter, facilitates the learner-content interaction in the form of a didactic text that encourages students through the process of designing and executing a research study. Additionally, the interactive instructor-led workshops provide ample learner-instructor interaction by providing motivation, organization, and counsel to the students through this process (Moore, 1989).

In this chapter, I examine the relevance of teaching the scientific process to non-science students and use the course Advanced Nonverbal Communication, taught in the Aarhus Summer University Program, as a case study. This chapter details the process of making the scientific process accessible to non-science students, fostering collaborative thinking through open educational resources (OER), and accomplishing these goals in a limited time frame. The assignment is described, and connections between the steps of the assignment and Bloom's taxonomy for learning are provided. The outcomes of the assignment are described, and the assessment is appraised for its applicability to other courses, fields, and modalities.

Focused Questions:

1. How might you apply this assignment to your course learning objectives and outcomes?
2. How can you apply observational research to your course?
3. Could you use this guide to adopt a different research methodology in your course, such as a survey, an interview series, or a content analysis?

Rationale

The undergraduate students in this chapter's international summer university course were from institutions throughout Europe, Asia, and North America. They were enrolled in academic programs, including adult education and personnel management, business administration and commercial law, civil engineering, finance, global management and manufacturing, and occupational therapy.

Some of these fields (e.g., occupational therapy) contain explicit instruction in scientific thinking. Others in this list do not have such a direct focus on scientific research methods, but the benefits of studying scientific thinking within these curricula are still acknowledged. For instance, while financial models can be produced by computer software, finance professors promote the teaching of the scientific method in order to adapt and interpret those models (Kane, 2004). The supply of readily available consumer data to large businesses has prompted an increased call within business schools to teach the scientific method, experimentation, and skills in synthesizing research findings from scholarly work.

Schools are also encouraged to provide students with assignments that require them to apply these scientific thinking skills (Tenney et al., 2021). In the sections that follow, I will expand on the benefits of teaching scientific thinking to undergraduate and graduate students across all academic disciplines and then explore the assignment itself.

Teaching Scientific Thinking Across Disciplines

In an article in *Scientific American,* Peter Salovey (2018), president of Yale University stated, "Knowledge is power but only if individuals are able to analyze and compare information against their personal beliefs, are willing to champion data-driven decision making over ideology, and have access to a wealth of research findings to inform policy discussions and decisions" (p. 11), highlighting the importance of fostering students' abilities as critical and creative thinkers who can make informed, evidence-driven decisions. Let us examine first what scientific methodology is and how it is connected to critical and creative thinking.

Scientific methodology is recognized as a collective standard of principles and processes that produce knowledge of the world by way of curiosity, critical thinking, empirical observations, and interpretation of those observations in a way that protects against cognitive bias (Gauch, 2003). Although wording and the number of stages may vary, the scientific process generally includes stages of asking a question, conducting research, forming and testing hypotheses, analyzing conclusions, and sharing findings.

Critical thinking speaks to the ability to assess statements (Ennis, 1964), engage in learning new material, problem-solving, and decision-making (Sternberg, 1986), and the capacity to recognize connections between statements (Mulnix, 2013). In a statement presented to the 8th Annual International Conference on Critical Thinking and Education Reform, Scriven and Paul (1987) defined critical thinking more thoroughly as "...the intellectually disciplined process of actively and skillfully conceptualizing, applying, analyzing, synthesizing, and/or evaluating information gathered from, or generated by, observation, experience, reflection, reasoning, or communication, as a guide to belief and action" (para. 3). Ultimately, critical thinking is an intentional, methodological process that fosters informed decision-making based on evidence rather than conjecture.

Scientific thinking is critical thinking. Every stage of the scientific process requires the researcher to think critically. To ask questions is to reflect on the world. Conducting research requires analyzing, synthesizing, and evaluating information. To develop a hypothesis entails drawing connections, and to test it requires problem-solving and observation. Analyzing and reporting the results necessitates evaluative assessment of the new information.

Despite the term creative thinking appearing in print over a decade before critical thinking, according to Google's N-Gram viewer, critical thinking quickly overtook creative thinking by the 1940s. This trend, which persisted into the 1990s, reflects a broader emphasis on teaching critical thinking skills over creative thinking skills (Puccio & Lohiser, 2020; Runco, 2007). But, creative thinking also has strong ties to the scientific process—creative thinking is applying one's imagination to make connections, envision and generate ideas, and bring them into being (Nielsen & Thurber, 2016; Osborn, 1979). At its root, creative thinking is a process—the result of dissonance in the mind between what is and what could be, which prompts the generation of something novel and useful (Stein, 1953). The Creative Problem Solving process (CPS) originated by Osborn and Parnes echoes scientific thinking with its four stages: (1) Clarify the problem, (2) Ideate potential ways for solving it, (3) Develop a workable solution, and (4) Implement that solution as an action plan. Within each of these stages, divergent thinking and convergent thinking occur. Divergence focuses on producing as much information or options as possible and convergence focuses on sifting through those choices for that which is most relevant and useful (Miller et al., 2011; Puccio et al., 2012).

Therefore, scientific thinking is also creative thinking. Inherent curiosity gives rise to asking questions and seeking their answers. Students who engage in scientific thinking *are* engaging in creative problem solving, with divergent and convergent thinking evident along the way. Stein (1953), in fact, speaks directly to creative thinking entailing the development and testing of hypotheses, as well as the need to communicate the novel output to others. The CPS is a process for developing new and workable solutions to problems based on evidence and observation (Puccio et al., 2012). It is reflected in the stages of conducting research, forming and testing hypotheses, analyzing conclusions, and sharing findings.

There is a place for scientific thinking across all academic disciplines, and the following project provides students from any educational background a taste of this process in a way that makes it fun, accessible, and rewarding.

Assessment Description

The assessment described in this chapter combines student-developed materials with an instructor-led narrative and is designed to be used in a concentrated 2-3 week period. It could also serve as a stand-alone unit or course. The assessment consists of a guide entitled *Research Projects for Beginners: A Guided Journey* and is intended to be used in a synchronous or asynchronous setting. This guide walks students through the scientific process in an easy-to-follow way, with each of the six stages of the scientific process broken down into steps that fall within the higher-order learning levels of Bloom's Taxonomy, with corresponding tasks within each step. All of these tasks ultimately coalesce into a research paper, completed in three parts—Research Question and Hypotheses (paper 1), Method and Rationale (paper 2), and Findings and Discussion (paper 3). Within the guide are three points at which students generate OER content. I created this assessment for Advanced Nonverbal Communication, taught in this case as a 3-week undergraduate course.

Advanced Nonverbal Communication is an undergraduate course constructed around the objectives of fostering an understanding of the evolutionary roots of nonverbal behavior and the effects of environment, territory, personal space, physical characteristics, gesture, posture, touch, facial expressions, eye behavior, and vocalics on human communication. The course topics are explored through a cross-cultural lens and from the perspective of applicability in a professional environment. Students learn to better interpret the nonverbal cues in the world around them and become more aware of the nonverbal messages they send. I teach the course for three weeks as part of the International Summer University program at Aarhus University, which started in 2010 with the vision to provide Aarhus students with the opportunity to gain international experiences at home while advancing their degrees, promote Aarhus University to international students through studying there for the summer, and foster internationalization through the offering of courses by international lecturers to a diverse student audience (T. F. Mortensen, personal communication, September 16, 2024).

To best meet the learning objectives of this course, with consideration of both the timeframe and diverse student backgrounds, I guide students through the scientific process, enabling them to conduct their own observational research by way of web cameras found on the website Earthcam.com and present those findings orally and in a final paper.

Making Scientific Thinking Accessible to Non-Science Students

Having established why scientific thinking benefits non-science students, the pedagogical challenge becomes making the scientific process accessible to them and preventing students from a variety of academic backgrounds from feeling daunted by the steps of an unfamiliar process in a concentrated timeline. The solution to this challenge was to take the "big thing" and turn it into multiple smaller things, presented in an easy-to-follow linear structure. Task-by-task, students encountered and executed the stages of research in scaffolded steps that tapped into their innate curiosity and the benefits of peer-to-peer learning. I structured the guide by combining the rigor of the scientific method with elements of creative problem-solving, presented in a narrative way.

The instructor-led guide is an OER published under a CC-BY license (see Appendix A). Table 1 provides an overview of the guide, the tasks within it, the corresponding stages of the scientific process, the levels of Bloom's taxonomy that each falls into, and the outcome produced in each step. Figure 1 shows a screenshot of the guide and the organizational outline or "document tabs" that enable easy navigation of this pageless document.

Figure 1: Screenshot of Guide's Organizational Outline

The guide breaks the scientific process into six stages and presents three OER documents constructed by the students for the collective benefit of their current peers and students in future offerings of the class. The benefits of OER are seen as a learner-to-learner interaction in that students benefit from the knowledge and guidance of their own peers (Moore, 1989).

Correlation of Steps to Bloom's Taxonomy

Each of the steps in the guide were crafted to fit within the higher orders of thinking within Bloom's revised taxonomy as described in Krathwohl (2002). For example, "developing a good query" fits within the Create cognitive process dimension of Bloom's revised taxonomy, as students might choose to generate their own original question at this stage. It also fits within the Applying dimension, as students may take a previously existing question and adapt it to their own interests. The overview of the guide in Table 1 shows where each of these steps fall within Bloom's revised taxonomy, demonstrating the higher orders of thinking that this research project promotes.

The guide walks students through all six steps of the scientific process, which are broken down into one or more steps, each containing one or more tasks. Along the way, the tasks help students write three portfolio assignments that ultimately form the building blocks of an entire research paper. The first portfolio assignment within the guide is an "Annotated

Bibliography." This assignment incorporates Stages 1-3 in the scientific process: *Ask a question, Do background research,* and *Develop a hypothesis,* and students complete nine tasks that lead them up to this paper. The second portfolio assignment within the guide is a "Methods and Rationale" paper. It incorporates Stage 4 in the scientific process: *Test your hypothesis,* and students complete six tasks in preparation for writing this paper. The third and final portfolio assignment within the guide is a "Findings and Conclusions" paper. It incorporates Stages 5-6 in the scientific process: *Analyze data* and *Report your findings,* and incorporates a total of six tasks. The following section details each element of this guide document:

- The STAGES of the scientific process, which are clarified as one or more STEPS
- The interactive TASK(S) within each step that students complete within the guided worksheet document
- The OER components that students develop together
- The portfolio assignment papers that students write, which eventually become the pieces of their final research paper.

For a detailed visual overview of this guide's design, see Table 1.

Table 1: *Guide Overview*

Scientific thinking stage	Steps within the guide for this stage	Where step fits in Bloom's taxonomy	Description of tasks related to the step within the guide	OER component within this step	Culmination portfolio paper:
1. Ask a question	Developing a good query	Applying; Create	*1. Students select a question* *2. Write their question*	Collaboration: Research Findings from previous years	
2. Do background research	Identifying constructs and variables	Analyze	*3. List constructs*		
	Finding scholarly research	Analyze	*4. List search strings*	Collaboration: Useful articles	Portfolio Paper #1: Research question, annotated bibliography, hypotheses
	Analyzing sources	Analyze; Create	*5. Create annotations*		
3. Develop a hypothesis	Creating a hypothesis	Create	*6. Indicate the independent and dependent variables* *7. Write the hypothesis* *8. Write the null hypothesis* *9. Draw on Tasks 1-8 to write Portfolio #1*		

Scientific thinking stage	Steps within the guide for this stage	Where step fits in Bloom's taxonomy	Description of tasks related to the step within the guide	OER component within this step	Culmination portfolio paper:
4. Test your hypothesis	Selecting your observational research setting	Evaluate	*1. Re-write hypotheses* *2. Record information about selected cameras*	Collaboration: Interesting cameras	Portfolio Paper #2: Methods, Rationale
	Designing your data collection system	Create	*3. Create data collection table*		
	Setting your observation times and duration	Create	*4. Answer questions about data collection times*		
	Collecting your data	Create	*5. Record data* *6. Draw on Tasks 1-5 to write Portfolio #2*		
5. Analyze and draw a conclusion	Explaining what you observed	Analyze	*1. Answer questions about patterns in observations* *2. Summarize findings*		Portfolio Paper #3: Findings, Discussion
	Interpreting what you observed	Evaluate	*3. Connect findings to annotated bib* *4. Review hypotheses* *5. Consider limitations* *6. Consider usefulness of study* *7. Draw on Tasks 1-6 to write Portfolio #3*		
6. Report your results	Communicating your findings in class	Create	*Unnumbered but described: Present in class*		
	Sharing your findings with future students	Create	*Unnumbered but described: Contribute to 3rd OER database*	Collaboration: Research findings	

The guide starts by explaining the document's layout, showing how the scientific process is depicted as a flowchart. Colored boxes represent the different stages in the scientific process, illustrated in Figure 2.

Figure 2: Color-coded Flowchart of the Scientific Process

Students are guided through the scientific process using a color-coded system. The process stages are associated with specific headings; the tasks they need to complete are highlighted in white boxes with red numbers. Specifically, students are introduced to how the stages of the scientific process correspond to color-coded headings that will walk them through a series of tasks and how to recognize the tasks in their white offset boxes with red numbers (see Figure 1). Then, students complete three portfolio assignments at key points during the process. Additionally, they are introduced to the "collaborate" directive, which appears in dark gray boxes, indicating moments when they will work together to create an OER component.

Stage 1: Ask a Question

The guide begins with Stage 1 of the scientific process: *Ask a question*. This stage is consolidated into one step: "Developing a good query." After a brief introduction to relay the connection between the scientific process and human curiosity, students are presented with a series of twelve questions. Task 1 in this step instructs students to choose one question that interests them the most. Task 2 invites them to adapt the question to their interests. This promotes individuality, freedom of thought, and the spirit of inquiry. However, pre-crafted questions may be useful for the student who is new to this process and may not know where to begin. They may end up adapting the question to better suit their interests and findings within the research as they progress through the tasks.

During Stage 1, students can also access the OER document they will encounter at the end of the research project. This document asks them to compile a short summary that includes their research question, hypotheses, methods, and findings. Students may use a question they find there as a springboard for their research. Details from previous students' assignments are rich enough to provide inspiration and cumulative knowledge-building without being overwhelming while also ensuring academic rigor by preventing them from entirely replicating another student's research methods.

Stage 2: Do Background Research

Next, students begin Stage 2: *Do background research*. Stage 2 contains three steps: "Identifying constructs and variables," "Finding scholarly research," and "Analyzing sources." The step "Identifying constructs and variables" contains Task 3, which encourages divergent thinking by listing as many words related to their research question that they may wish to research further. The goal is to enable students to think of synonyms for the constructs in their question, which will aid in locating research articles and, later, identifying variables to formulate their hypotheses.

The step "Finding scholarly research" begins with an introduction to Google Scholar and a library's periodical databases. The guide demonstrates to students how to type in a search string and access the search results as open-access PDFs or hyperlinks connected through a library database. Task 4 in this step asks students to create search strings related to their question and test them in Google Scholar or their library's search page. Students are helped to understand that they may not find articles that speak to their topic specifically, but they may find ones that will inform them by building a constellation of perspectives on the topic.

Next, the "Finding scholarly research" step includes the first student-developed OER component, where students contribute key sources they have found to a Google Sheet that lists the year, authors, title, hyperlink, type of source, and key topics. This creates a compendium of screened sources relevant to their project and potentially to the projects of their peers. Figure 3 shows a screenshot demonstrating how students (names redacted) have populated the sheet.

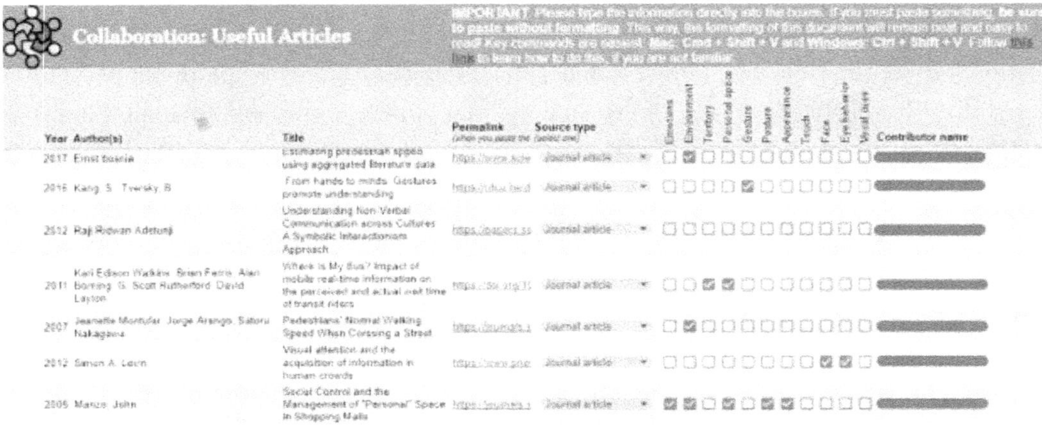

Figure 3: Screenshot of OER Collaboration Document with Student Entries

The final step in this stage, "Analyzing sources," helps students begin to compile the elements of an annotated bibliography as a method for reviewing and analyzing sources. While a literature review offers a deeper synthesis of themes across sources, past experiences show that an annotated bibliography proved to be a more approachable way for students new to academic research. This step explains annotated bibliographies and citations with color-coded examples, hyperlinked sources, and examples of annotated paragraphs. Task 5 within this step provides color-coded boxes (see Figure 4) with explanatory text that enables students to begin writing their annotated bibliographies, consisting of a citation, a summative paragraph, and a research connection and critique paragraph.

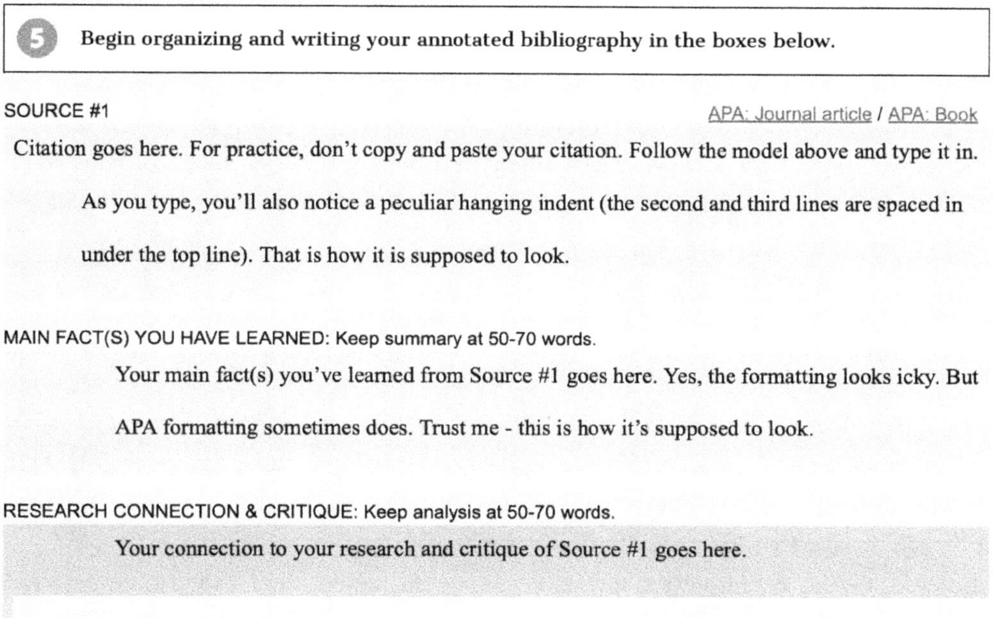

5 **Begin organizing and writing your annotated bibliography in the boxes below.**

SOURCE #1 APA: Journal article / APA: Book

Citation goes here. For practice, don't copy and paste your citation. Follow the model above and type it in. As you type, you'll also notice a peculiar hanging indent (the second and third lines are spaced in under the top line). That is how it is supposed to look.

MAIN FACT(S) YOU HAVE LEARNED: Keep summary at 50-70 words.

Your main fact(s) you've learned from Source #1 goes here. Yes, the formatting looks icky. But APA formatting sometimes does. Trust me - this is how it's supposed to look.

RESEARCH CONNECTION & CRITIQUE: Keep analysis at 50-70 words.

Your connection to your research and critique of Source #1 goes here.

Figure 4: Screenshot of Annotated Bibliography Organization

Stage 3: Develop a Hypothesis

Stage 3 is also consolidated into one step: "Creating a hypothesis." Students are given definitions and examples of independent and dependent variables. Now that they are more informed on their topics through a review of the literature, students isolate one key independent and dependent variable in Task 6. While they could identify multiple variables, they are encouraged to keep their inquiry limited to focus on just one of each.

With DV and IV prepared, students now construct a hypothesis (H_1) and a null hypothesis (H_0) in Tasks 7 and 8. When applicable, students are asked to generate the opposite wording of their hypothesis to serve as a second hypothesis (e.g., H_1: In a more crowded environment, strangers acknowledge each other less frequently, and H_2: In a less crowded environment, strangers acknowledge each other more frequently). Although this action may seem superfluous, I have found that requiring students to analyze their observational framework that identifies two different variations of the same factors encourages more detailed observation that helps prevent confirmation bias.

First Portfolio Assignment: Ask a Question, Do Background Research, Develop a Hypothesis

The guide now presents students with directions for the first portfolio assignment (Task 9), which systematically explains how to compile each Task from the stages above into a paper. Students' research questions developed in Tasks 1 and 2 in Stage 1 (Ask a question) are incorporated into a paragraph in which the research question is appropriately introduced. The citations for the sources they found and the accompanying annotative paragraphs from Tasks 3-5 in Stage 2 (Do background research) become the annotated bibliography. Finally, the hypotheses they developed through Tasks 6-8 in Stage 3 (Develop a hypothesis) become a closing paragraph, which draws clear connections between how students progressed from research question to hypotheses and introduces the hypotheses in appropriate detail. After the directions for the first portfolio assignment, the guide instructs students to stop at that point.

Stage 4: Test Your Hypothesis

The next part of the guide introduces Stage 4 of the scientific process: *Test your hypothesis*. This stage is split into four steps: "Selecting your observational research setting," "Designing your data collection system," "Setting your observation times and duration," and "Collecting your data." There are a total of six Tasks across these steps.

The website EarthCam is the primary source of cameras for this assignment series, although students generated options from other websites, as well. EarthCam is an atlas of sorts of live streaming (and archived footage from) web cameras around the world. Some cameras provide a distance-perspective of people's behavior (e.g., Moscow Skyline Cam, 2024), and others provide a closer view, like a city sidewalk (e.g., Times Square Street Cam, 2024) or a close-up view of people dining in a café (e.g., Miami News Cafe, 2024). These cameras are usually found in areas of prevalent tourism and allow people to explore the world, fostering a sense of connection and community (EarthCam, 2024). Before being introduced to EarthCam, students rewrite their hypotheses in Task 1. Then, EarthCam is introduced to students. In Task 2, students explore the site and begin compiling information about cameras that might provide them with a viable field for conducting observations to help them explore their hypotheses.

After Task 2, students encounter the second OER component. Students access an editable Google Sheet where they share interesting cameras they have found. The checkboxes within the sheet indicate what elements are visible in the cameras (e.g., crosswalks, benches, foot traffic) and what textbook topics the camera may pertain to (e.g., personal space, gesture, face). In this way, students construct a database of useful cameras for their peers and future students in the class to use as a resource. A screenshot is shown in Figure 5, demonstrating how students (names redacted) have populated the sheet.

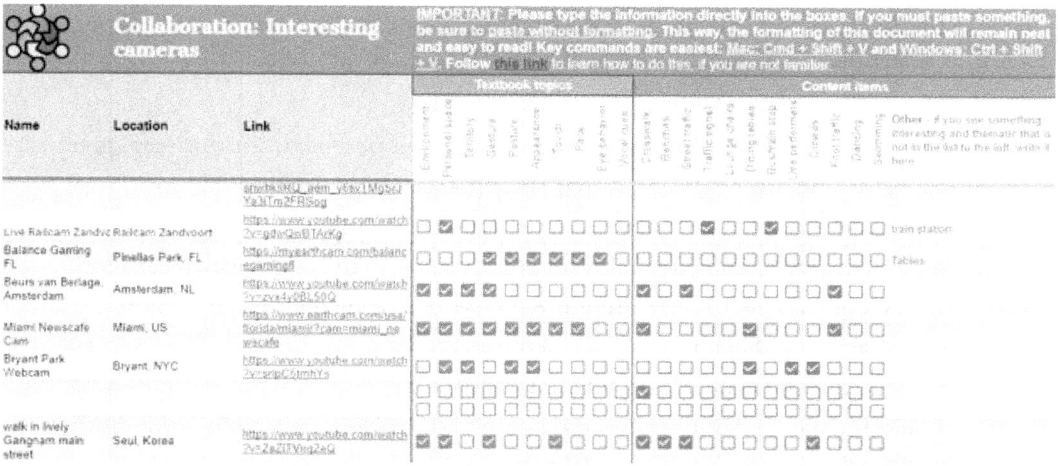

Figure 5: Screenshot of OER Collaboration Document with Student Entries

The next steps in Stage 4 are "Designing your data collection system" and "Setting your observation times and duration." These steps emphasize the importance of building a sound methodology that prevents confirmation bias. Students create a table to record their data in Task 3 and identify the time of day and duration of their observations in Task 4.

The final step in this stage is "Collecting your data." In Task 5, students implement their plan by conducting their observations in and out of class time and keeping detailed, organized records of what they see. Students are encouraged to conduct enough observations until they begin to see patterns emerge and can recognize the frequency and consistency of events.

Second Portfolio Assignment: Methods and Rationale for Testing Your Hypothesis

The second portfolio assignment is a methods paper. The directions show students how Task 1, in which they rewrote their hypotheses, becomes an introduction. Tasks 2-4 enable them to describe in detail the way they set out to collect observations. Students name the cameras and describe the vantage point afforded, the time and duration of their observations, and how they recorded their data. The second section of the paper is their rationale, where students draw connections between their methodology and those they read about during their review of the literature.

Stage 5: Analyze Data and Draw Conclusions

Stage 5 is *Analyze and draw conclusions*, which contains two steps: "Explaining what you observed" and "Interpreting what you observed".

Task 1 in "Explaining what you observed" guides students through questions to answer based on their table of collected data, including "What patterns emerged across your observations?" and "Did you see anything that surprised you?". Then, they are shown how to synthesize their findings, demonstrating the difference between a "data dump" and a well organized data display. Finally, students summarize their findings into up to five key points of interest in Task 2.

The second step in this stage is "Interpreting what you observed." In this step, great care is taken to ensure students understand that their data are not generalizable to a larger population. Instead, the data are descriptive rather than inferential, and students must express their findings accordingly. This step helps students analyze patterns identified earlier through comparison and contrasts with their literature review, driven by their original thinking rather than numerical analysis. Therefore, Task 3 requires students to explicitly list their findings and compare or contrast them to a finding in a source they reviewed. In Task 4, they list their hypotheses and indicate whether they were supported (fully or partially). Study limitations are explained, and they compile a list of limitations in Task 5. Finally, they indicate what makes their study useful, interesting, important, or relevant in Task 6.

Stage 6: Report Your Results

Stage 6, *Report your results*, contains two steps: "Communicating your findings in class" and "Sharing your findings with future students."

First, "Communicating your findings in class" includes a brief presentation in which students state their hypotheses, highlight the essence of their methods, and present their most interesting findings. The comparison of this class event to a research conference is played up only to the level at which it affects a fun, convivial atmosphere rather than to place upon it the pressure of an oral exam. This class event could lend itself well to an event within a pre-existing campus community research forum.

The final step, "Sharing your findings with future students," constitutes the third and final OER component. Students enter a summarized version of their research question, hypotheses, methods, and primary findings on a Google Sheet, knowing that future students may refer to it during Stage 1, *Ask a question*. Students are encouraged, but not required, to leave their contact information should students wish to reach out to them.

Third Portfolio Assignment: Analyze Data, Draw Conclusions, and Report Your Results

The final portfolio assignment is a Conclusions paper. The guide directions show how Tasks 1 and 2 become a "Findings" section, in which students describe what they saw objectively, in narrative and table form. Tasks 3-6 become a "Discussion" section in which students interpret their findings based on the literature and assess the limitations and usefulness of their study.

Debrief

By way of a template that simply guides students through the result of stitching the three portfolio projects together, students submit a research paper at the end of the three weeks of guided instruction. A key element of the 2024 course was the introduction of new open educational resources (OER) materials, which included a compilation of research sources and EarthCam hyperlinks. Feedback from students' final papers indicates that these resources were useful in supporting their research. Many students incorporated multiple cameras and sources into their work, demonstrating that the resources provided a valuable foundation. However, it is notable that the integration of these materials was not so extensive that students relied entirely on the work of their peers, suggesting a balanced use of the resources.

Next summer, I will incorporate the third OER component—the database of student research questions, method summary, and key findings—into the *Ask a question* stage of the research project, as described above. This will allow the work of the 2024 cohort to directly benefit the 2025 cohort by providing a structured resource for their research inquiries. By incorporating this student-generated content into the learning process, the course will support current students and foster a sense of collaboration and continuity between classes. This evolution of the OER materials aims to enhance the collaborative and cumulative nature of the research project, further enriching the student experience.

Appraisal

A student exit survey yielded supportive comments about the efficacy of the guide in teaching the research process to non-science students. One student wrote:

> The guided worksheet was immensely helpful in helping me write my first research paper without feeling intimidated by it. Breaking it down into bite-sized sections helped to organize thoughts and even left me surprised at how long the paper was by the end after only doing small parts at a time.

This feedback highlights the value of breaking complex tasks into manageable steps, which helped reduce anxiety and encouraged steady progress. The student's surprise at the length of the final paper reflects the guide's effectiveness in facilitating incremental progress, ultimately empowering students to complete a full research paper with confidence.

This project could serve as a stand-alone module within a larger course or could be similarly integrated into a shorter class term like this one. The project itself could reasonably be executed within a one-week "workshop" time frame consisting of five 3-hour instructional/ guided workshop periods followed by student work periods outside of class or built within the workshop. The goal of offering the overview of this assignment series is to demonstrate its value both for its applicability as a stand-alone accelerated course or as a stand-alone module that could be implemented within other courses for which the scientific method or the concept of observational research might be appropriate.

The guided project series described in this chapter can be adapted to various research methods in other disciplines, especially if given the time to procure IRB approval from the home university. For example, the process could be applied to creating a survey, conducting interviews or focus groups, content analyses, or even executing a simple lab experiment.

Results from the student survey also suggested that the OER components were valuable, with 18 of the 22 students surveyed reporting them to be "useful" or "very useful," with "useful" being defined as enhancing their comprehension of the topic of nonverbal communication. In addition, nearly 50 unique peer review sources were compiled into the first OER document, "Collaboration: Useful Articles," and seven alternative cameras were added to the second OER document, "Collaboration: Interesting Cameras." The final OER document, "Collaboration: Research Findings," in which students contributed a summary of their research, was less populated, with five students detailing their studies and four including their contact information for future students to contact them. Two observations are worth noting: (1) Greater OER document completion might be attainable by attaching a small incentive, and (2) The OER document served as a springboard for wider, less-documented student collaboration.

Years of teaching research methods and overseeing numerous student projects have shown me that a successful, simple analysis of a small amount of data does more for a beginner student's self-assuredness than trying to manage and interpret a large amount of data with complex analyses. Cooking classes do not begin with the hardest recipes for a reason. Using this analogy, some students in this class eventually tackle complex projects—the bœuf bourguignon—but even the most experienced chef begins with a basic omelet. This project strives to yield successful, confidence-building "omelets" through simple observational studies, ensuring students understand the basics of the scientific process supported by their peers.

References

EarthCam. (2024). *About EarthCam*. https://www.earthcam.com/company/aboutus.php

Ennis, R. H. (1964). A definition of critical thinking. *The Reading Teacher*, 17(8), 599-612. https://www.jstor.org/stable/20197828

Gauch, H. G. (2003). *Scientific method in practice*. Cambridge University Press.

Kane, S. (2004). Scientific methods in finance. *International Review of Financial Analysis*, 13(2004), 105-118. https://doi.org/10.1016/j.irfa.2004.01.003

Krathwohl, D. R. (2002). A revision of Bloom's Taxonomy: An overview. *Theory into Practice*, 41(4), 212-218. https://doi.org/10.1207/s15430421tip4104_2

Miami News Cafe. (2024). *Enjoy the sights of Miami!* https://www.earthcam.com/usa/florida/miami/?cam=miami_newscafe

Miller, B., Vehar, J., Firestien, R., Thurber, S., & Nielsen, D. (2011). *Creativity unbound: An Introduction to creative process.* FourSight LLC.

Moore, M. G. (1989). Editorial: Three types of interaction. *American Journal of Distance Education, 3*(2), 1-6. https://doi.org/10.3200/CTCH.56.4.219-224

Moscow Today. (2024). *Live from Moscow!* https://www.earthcam.com/world/russia/moscow/?cam=moscow_hd

Mulnix, J. W. (2013). Thinking critically about critical thinking. *Educational Philosophy and Theory, 44*(5), 464-479. https://doi.org/10.1111/j.1469-5812.2010.00673.x

Nielsen, D., & Thurber, S. (2016). *The secret of the highly creative thinker: How to make connections others don't.* BIS Publishers.

Osborn, A. F. (1979). *Applied imagination.* Charles Scribner's Sons.

Puccio, G. J., & Lohiser, A. (2020). The case for creativity in higher education: Preparing students for life and work in the 21st century. *Kindai Management Review/The Institute for Creative Management and Innovation,* Kinki University, 8, 30-47.

Puccio, G. J., Mance, M., Barbero Switalski, L., & Reali, P. (2012). *Creativity rising: Creative thinking and creative problem solving in the 21st century.* ICSC Press.

Runco, M. A. (2007). *Creativity: Theories and Themes: Research. Development and Practice.* Elsevier Academic Press.

Salovey, P. (2018, June). We should teach all students, in every discipline, to think like scientists. *Scientific American, 318*(6), 11-12. https://www.scientificamerican.com/article/we-should-teach-all-students-in-every-discipline-to-think-like-scientists/

Scriven, M., & Paul, R. (1987). Defining critical thinking. In *The Foundation for Critical Thinking.* https://www.criticalthinking.org/pages/defining-critical-thinking/766

Stein, M. I. (1953). Creativity and culture. *Journal of Psychology, 36,* 31–322.https://doi.org/10.1080/00223980.1953.9712897

Sternberg, R. J. (1986). Critical thinking: Its nature, measurement, and improvement. *National Institution of Education,* 1-37. https://eric.ed.gov/?id=ED272882

Tenney, E. R., Costa, E., & Watson, R. M. (2021, June 16). *Why business schools need to teach experimentation.* Harvard Business Review. https://hbr.org/2021/06/why-business-schools-need-to-teach-experimentation

Times Square Street Cam. (2024). *Live from NYC's Times Square!* https://www.earthcam.com/usa/newyork/timessquare/?cam=tsstreet

Chapter 3 Appendix

Appendix A

Here is a link to the guided worksheet, Research Projects for Beginners: A Guided Journey. Click the link above to be prompted to make your own copy of the Guided Research Worksheets document described in this chapter. Once you have made your copy, it is yours to adapt as you wish. Feel free to make the narrative your own, adjust the assignment parameters to work within the scope of your course, the research methodology to best meet your learning objectives, etc.

Here are some important usage notes:

1. Read the guide carefully to adapt the content to your course and needs. This guide was written for a specific course, and not all of the content may be applicable to your course. This guide requires adaptation.
2. Each of the three Collaborate boxes have a hyperlink attached to the icon picture on the left side of the dark gray box (the model in the introduction does not). Those hyperlink prompts you to make a copy of the Collaborate worksheet. Once you have made your copy, create your "sharing" link and embed it into the icon picture. To embed a link into a picture in Google Docs, click the image, and select "Insert link" from the menu bar.
3. When your guide is ready for student use, share it with them by clicking the "Share" button. Select "Anyone with the link" and choose "Editor" from the drop-down menu. Once you have copied your link, paste it into a notepad or similar, and delete "edit?usp=sharing" from the end of the code. Replace it with the word "copy". This enables students to click that link and make their own copy of the guided worksheets.

If you have any additional questions about using this guide, please contact the author at alohiser@ur.rochester.edu.

4. Reinventing Exam Question Assessments in the Age of AI to Reflect Diverse Voices and Promote Critical Thinking

Kelly Soczka Steidinger, M.A.

Chapter Learning Objectives:

- Incorporate an assessment into course curriculum that uses artificially intelligent large language models to increase students' technological proficiency and literacy.
- Implement an assessment that promotes students' awareness of and sensitivity to diverse perspectives and experiences.
- Identify the value of student-constructed content by utilizing renewable and openly licensed assessments to benefit the broader educational community.

Chapter Overview

This chapter explores how undergraduate students use generative artificially intelligent (AI) models, such as Google's Gemini, ChatGPT, and Claude, to formulate scenario-based multiple-choice questions with a critical perspective. Since artificially intelligent large language models (LLMs) are infused with inherent human bias, hallucinations, and occasional structural flaws, I created an assessment that asks students to critically review and revise AI-generated questions to ensure they accurately reflected current course content and authentically represented their perspectives. To promote deep learning, students justify the accuracy of the correct answers and rank the plausibility of incorrect answers, citing peer-reviewed course materials to support their reasoning. Additionally, students add authenticity and humanize questions by creatively revising the contextual details of the questions with a focus on diversity, equity, and inclusion (DEI). The newly revised student multiple-choice questions are compiled and amalgamated into digital learning objects for the future use of students and openly licensed for public consumption as an open pedagogy project.

This chapter introduces the AI multiple-choice summative assessment that familiarizes students with LLMs, enhances the understanding of course content, and promotes inclusive exam design. Next, the chapter covers the academic benefits of the assessment, offers guidance on adoption into the course curriculum, and strategies for reusing revised questions in openly licensed digital resources for future students or the public. The chapter concludes with an overview of the assessment results, limitations, and alternative applications.

Focused Questions:

1. How can students use AI to advance their critical-analytical thinking skills?
2. How can you revise staple assessments in your academic discipline to enable AI skill-building while continuing to develop learners' higher-order thinking skills?
3. How can you leverage AI tools to enhance student learning and develop AI literacy skills?
4. How can you reinvent assessments to incorporate diversity, equity, and inclusion principles to strengthen student unity and spur creativity?
5. How can you integrate renewable assessments in your course curriculum to encourage student engagement and openly license student-constructed content to benefit future students or the community?

Rationale

With the advent of the 2022 public release of generative artificial intelligence, educators have been thrust into a new, continually changing technological landscape that directly impacts student skill development in higher education. According to Zeide (2019), AI is "the attempt to create machines that do things previously only possible through human cognition" (p. 31). Bowen and Watson (2024) also offer that AI "refers to the ability of computer systems to mimic human intelligence" (p. 16). Overnight assessments that were staples of the higher education classroom that assessed student cognition through writing, such as the "term paper," became obsolete. The rapid development and adoption of generative AI technologies, as highlighted by the 2022 public release, necessitated a shift in how educators approach student skill development in higher education.

While humans have been interacting with AI for years, such as interfacing with predictive text, facial recognition, and GPS navigation systems, the release of "generative" AI in the form of large language models (LLMs) to the public is a novel advancement that impacts numerous industries, including academia (Zeide, 2019). Unlike prior forms of AI, generative LLMs go beyond pattern recognition and can create new content, including computer code, text, images, and videos (Xia et al., 2024). Since LLMs can generate unique ideas, draw conclusions, and find answers, how should instructors modify curriculum, assessments, and classroom practices to ensure students continue to advance their cognition and critical thinking skills? Constructing assessments that stimulate students' critical thinking will be a new challenge for educators in the 21st century. This chapter provides a solution to the dilemma by instilling students with AI literacy skills.

AI Literacy Framework

The definition of AI literacy continues to mature as technology evolves. At the core of AI literacy is the "understanding and capability to interact effectively with AI technology" (Walter, 2024, p. 11). Moreover, the concept of AI literacy encompasses more than just the technical aspects of interfacing with AI but also includes the recognition of the social and ethical ramifications of AI. A more nuanced approach to understanding AI literacy integration into the curriculum can be better understood when educators consider Ng et al.'s (2021) framework of AI literacy. This framework entails four levels of understanding that align with the cognitive domains of Bloom's Taxonomy. These levels, from lowest to highest levels of cognition, include:

1. Students will "know and understand" how to use basic AI applications and operations.
2. Students will "use and apply" AI concepts or skills in various scenarios.
3. Students will "evaluate and create" using higher-order thinking skills with generative AI models.
4. Students will "evaluate" AI ethics, which encourages students to consider ethical principles such as fairness, equity, accountability, and safety when using AI applications.

The AI multiple-choice assessment detailed in this chapter meets the four levels of Ng et al.'s (2021) framework. When completing the assignment, students use factor one by writing prompts and soliciting multiple-choice questions and responses from AI models. Next, students use their knowledge of AI within the "scenario" or context of exam question construction. The third factor is met when students evaluate and revise questions using Bloom's higher-order thinking skills, including analysis, evaluation, and critical thinking. The fourth and final level is met when students evaluate and revise questions because they consider social norms and apply inclusive principles.

Since AI doesn't interact with the external world, humans need to validate the authenticity of the information being generated by AI. One drawback of generative LLMs is the inability to detect human bias or stereotypes that may be present in large data sets from which chatbots pull information and provide it to users (Herder, 2023). AI presents correct and incorrect data equally, without any limitations, which results in marginalized persons and groups being underrepresented in solutions AI offers users (Herder, 2023; Leffer, 2023). Likewise, new research argues that humans may learn, reproduce, and carry this bias into offline interactions (Leffer, 2023). Thus, the need to teach AI literacy and focus on exposing and correcting this bias is imperative.

Recognizing the importance of AI literacy and the need to mitigate bias, I sought to create an assessment that would not only challenge students but also prepare them for the AI-driven future. To achieve this, I center the assessment on constructivist principles and critical thinking, which are skills essential to developing meaningful problem-solving abilities. Constructivism is an educational philosophy that educators use to design learning activities, assessments, and knowledge-acquisition strategies. A key principle of constructivism is learners actively cultivate knowledge for themselves (Schunk, 2020; Simpson, 2002). Moreover, constructivism has influenced instructional delivery and curriculum creation by proposing learners actively engage with course content through "manipulation of materials and social interaction" (Schunk, 2020, p. 316). For instance, when students write AI prompts and revise multiple-choice questions to reflect their perspectives, they manipulate course content, which improves critical thinking and content retention.

Exogenous Perspective of Constructivism

An additional and equally important constructivist principle embedded into the AI multiple-choice questions assessment is the exogenous perspective of constructivism. The exogenous perspective maintains the "assumption that knowledge is derived from one's environment and, in that sense, can be said to be learned" (Moshman, 1982, p. 373). Further, Moshman (1982) argues that the construction of knowledge is a reconstruction of information, relationships, and observed patterns found in students' external reality, where they acquire knowledge and skills through experiences, models, and teaching. When revising AI-generated questions, students learn course content by reconstructing their perception of reality by exemplifying human characteristics. Students demonstrate competency in their knowledge and skills through question revision. Additionally, Schunk (2020) adds, "Knowledge is accurate to the extent that it reflects that reality" (p. 316). When learners revise AI multiple-choice questions to focus on representing authentic human diversity, they construct a more accurate reflection of human reality and increase their knowledge about themselves and others.

Employing an assessment that asks students to revise multiple-choice questions through the lens of diversity, equity, and inclusion (DEI) exercises students' critical thinking. By embracing this assessment approach, students use critical thinking to "analyze questions, evaluate different perspectives, and create reasoned arguments" (Walter, 2024, p. 34). When completing the assessment, students practice:

1. "analyzing" and "evaluating" AI-generated questions to identify and replace AI bias, stereotypes, and underrepresentation.
2. "creating reasoned arguments" when justifying the accuracy of the AI's identified correct answers.
3. applying critical thinking when ranking the incorrect answer choices and providing "reasoned arguments" for their rankings.

Another method to stimulate critical thinking skills in the AI multiple-choice assessment involves asking students to write logical arguments to validate the correct answers and the incorrect answer ranking to the constructed questions (Harvard, 2020). There are several reasons to require students to identify where they located evidence to justify the questions' correct answers, including:

1. To increase students' AI literacy skills by highlighting the importance of using peer-reviewed materials to check the accuracy of AI-generated content since LLMs can hallucinate and provide skewed data that could lead to "discriminatory conclusions against underrepresented groups" (Walter, 2024, p. 12).
2. To guarantee the newly revised questions contain course concepts and theories that align with the course's current materials.
3. To encourage students to think critically and avoid using AI to generate explanations and answer rationales.

By building logical arguments and revising multiple-choice questions, students use creativity, critical thinking, and AI literacy skills.

Creating Renewable Assessments

The final purpose of the AI multiple-choice question assessment is to create a renewable assignment aligned with Open Pedagogy principles. As Wiley and Hilton (2018) define, renewable assessments "both support an individual student's learning and result in new or improved open educational resources that benefit the broader community of learners" (p. 137). Conversely, disposable assignments, seen only by the instructor, often hold little value for students beyond the experience and are frequently disliked by instructors to grade (Jhangiani, 2017). To benefit the wider community of learners and to extend beyond the individual student's experience, a renewable assessment is not "disposed of," and instead, the student's new content is reused (Wiley & Hilton, 2018). Wiley and Hilton (2018) also specify that students should create, revise, or remix a "renewable" assessment. Grounded in constructivist principles, the results of the AI multiple-choice assessment are openly licensed, shared, and offer further value. The AI multiple-choice assignment was designed as a renewable assessment based on constructivist philosophy, benefiting future students and the public. To be renewable, the revised multiple-choice questions are reused in future course materials, such as quizzes, exams, and reusable digital learning objects. According to Churchill (2007), learning objects (LOs) are designed for educational purposes, are digital, and reusable. In Churchill's (2007) taxonomy of learning objects, the researcher also identifies various typologies of LOs, including practice objects.

Practice learning objects, such as the exam questions discussed in this chapter, allow students to rehearse procedures, drag-and-drop objects, play games, and answer quiz questions (Churchill, 2007). By utilizing practice digital learning objects, learners interact with course concepts and self-test their understanding of new knowledge. Practice quizzes using digital learning objects allow learners to participate in "practicing the retrieval of learned information," which strengthens "the consolidation of learners' mental representation and hence long-term retention" (Roelle et al., 2022, p. 142). Thus, inserting newly constructed students' questions from their completed AI assignments into digital learning objects as practice quizzes will enhance future student exam performance and increase long-term retention of course information.

Assessment Description

This AI multiple-choice revision assessment was infused into a rural community college's Introduction to Psychology course curriculum. After assessment completion, students should be able to:

1. Construct AI prompts to generate scenario-based multiple-choice questions based on course theories and concepts.
2. Evaluate AI-constructed multiple-choice questions for accuracy, structure, and bias.
3. Apply theoretical perspectives to hypothetical scenarios when revising AI responses.
4. Apply accurate representations of DEI principles by revising contextual details and language in questions.
5. Justify the accuracy of the AI multiple-choice questions utilizing critical thinking skills and peer-reviewed course materials.
6. Write logical arguments to support the ranking of incorrect answers.

Before or in conjunction with discussing this assignment with students, instructors should provide direct instruction on bias in AI and inclusive language. Instructors should furnish students with examples of biased and corrective language to confirm learners can identify AI language that needs revision. A student resource for identifying and revising biased language is the American Psychological Association's *Inclusive Language Guide*. The guide describes inclusive language and terminology related to equity and power, person-first and identity-first language, and microaggressions (American Psychological Association, 2023). Additionally, the guide provides students with practical explanations and corrective examples in useful charts for quick reference.

After direct instruction on inclusive language, instructors should demonstrate where to find AI models and how to construct effective AI prompts. Since ChatGPT and Google's Gemini are generative LLMs designed for general public use and offer basic services for free, students can use these models. I prefer to use Google's Gemini because many students already have existing Google accounts, and Google provides accessible tutorials.[1]

When students begin the assessment, their first step is to write a prompt asking the LLMs to generate scenario-based multiple-choice questions. Learners then take a screenshot of the AI-generated response to provide the instructor with a copy of the student's prompt and question before learners revise it.[2] Students should be advised to include in their prompt the educational level of the audience for which the question is being designed (undergraduate university student, graduate student, etc.) and the course subject, theory, or course concept on which the question is being written.

Next, students use peer-reviewed course materials, such as textbooks, instructor-generated course slides, or journal articles, to check and justify the accuracy of the correct answers to the LLM-generated questions. Students then write a paragraph rationale to explain why the answer is correct or incorrect and identify the course materials they used to locate evidence to prove the accuracy of the AI's answers. After confirming the accuracy of the correct answer, students review the remaining answer choices, rank them from most to least plausible, and then defend and explain their rankings (Harvard, 2020), justifying their answers using course materials. Students must supply a page and paragraph number from the course textbook or the PowerPoint slide number to verify and provide evidence of their correct and incorrect answer rationales.

In the final step of the assessment, students revise the AI-generated questions to portray lived experience, eliminate bias, and increase diversity by adding contextual details to the scenario. For instance, students add diverse biographical information, such as names, ages, and locations, humanizing the question's context. The question scenarios should be no longer than 4 sentences, and the details should remain significant to the question so as not to distract from the correct answer. Likewise, details should not distract or mislead the reader from

1. AI tutorials include: Google's Gemini, FAQs, and how to write effective prompts.

2. For lower-level course students, I would also suggest providing directions on how to take screenshots. Tutorials for taking screenshots using a PC, a Google Chromebook, or a Mac computer.

answering the question successfully. An example set of assignment directions and grading rubric for students is provided in Appendix A. Then, Appendix B contains a sample of a completed student assignment that I shared with the students.

When students revise their questions, they should use inclusive language and construct a scenario portraying themselves. For example, Mid-State Technical College student Cassie Hucke exemplifies how her role as a non-generational student mother contributed to integrating an intergenerational perspective into her revised question. Figure 1 is an example of the AI-generated question before the student's revision.

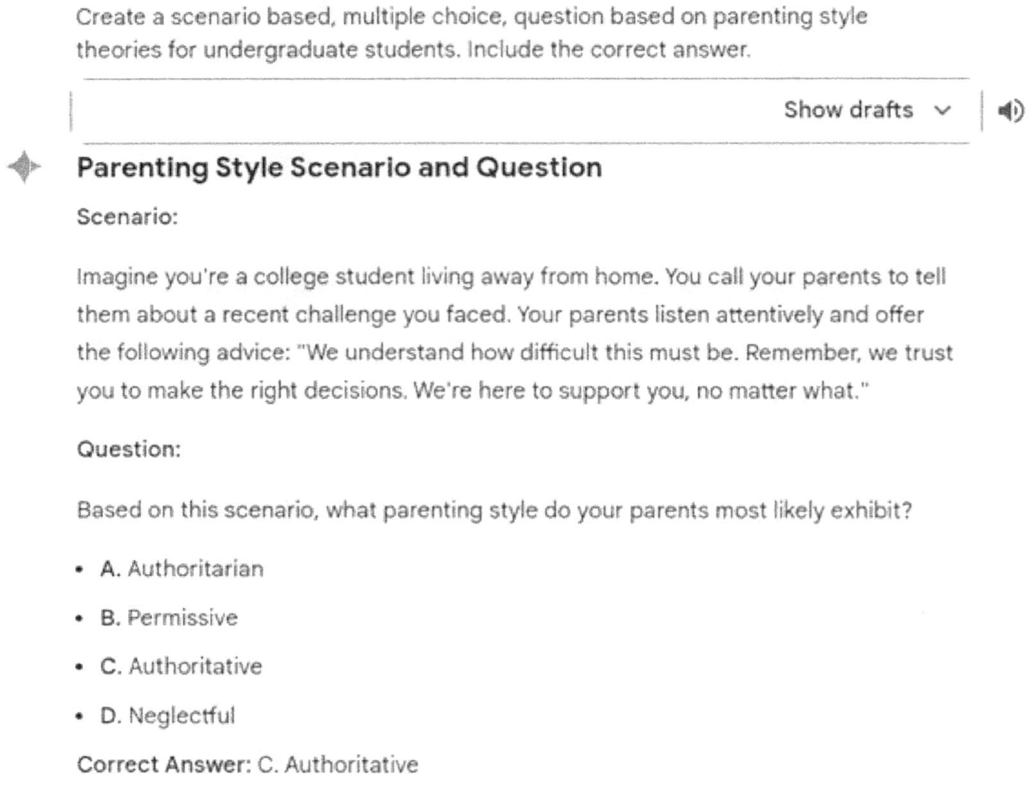

Create a scenario based, multiple choice, question based on parenting style theories for undergraduate students. Include the correct answer.

Show drafts ∨ ◀)

◆ Parenting Style Scenario and Question

Scenario:

Imagine you're a college student living away from home. You call your parents to tell them about a recent challenge you faced. Your parents listen attentively and offer the following advice: "We understand how difficult this must be. Remember, we trust you to make the right decisions. We're here to support you, no matter what."

Question:

Based on this scenario, what parenting style do your parents most likely exhibit?

- A. Authoritarian

- B. Permissive

- C. Authoritative

- D. Neglectful

Correct Answer: C. Authoritative

Figure 1: Image of AI-Generated Question Prior to Student Revision

Figure 2 presents Cassie Hucke's depiction of herself as a mother within the context of her revised question.

Cassie is now an adult learner going back to school while she has kids of her own. After she got her kids on the bus and was getting ready to go to class herself, she called her mother crying about how everything went wrong during the morning. Her mother told her to take a deep breath, told her she believed in her and to prioritize her morning, so when she gets to class she can focus on herself, her future, and her kids. Based on this information, which type of parenting style did Cassie's mother demonstrate?

○ **a.** Authoritative

○ **b.** Permissive

○ **c.** Authoritarian

○ **d.** Neglectful

Check Answer

Figure 2: Image of Cassie Hucke's Revised Multiple-Choice Question

Another student example, Kyle Koran, revised his question to include a cultural reference to the underage drinking problem in parts of Wisconsin. His question is revealed in Figure 3.

Mateo is a parent who desires to be a friend to his child. Mateo caught his child drinking with friends, instead of punishing his child, Mateo told the child not to drive, and not to get too drunk. Mateo feels that it is a learning experience for his child. Which of the following describes Mateo's parenting skills?

○ **a.** Uninvolved Parenting

○ **b.** Permissive

○ **c.** Authoritarian

○ **d.** Authoritative

Check Answer

Figure 3: Image of Kyle Koran's Revised Multiple-Choice Question

When students submit their completed assessment documents, they are also asked to submit a short Google Form to record their preferences regarding repurposing their newly revised questions. The survey asks students if they are willing to share their newly constructed questions with future students as an openly licensed digital learning object and if they would like their names to be included below the question. Students can share their work anonymously, with their names attached, or not at all. A sample of the survey questions is provided in Appendix C.

After students submit their work, I identify and compile exemplary questions for incorporation into future quizzes, exams, and digital learning objectives. I only chose questions that students identified as sharable in their survey responses. A student survey I conducted revealed that students overwhelmingly agreed to share their work with future students: 11 students indicated they were excited to contribute to future learning, 14 indicated they were satisfied to be a part of the process, six were neutral, and zero indicated they were hesitant to share their work or were not interested in sharing. These results suggest that most students were willing to share their work with others. Yet, surprisingly, most students wished to remain anonymous if their questions were shared online, with 25 students indicating they wanted to remain anonymous and only six indicating they wanted their names associated with their work.

Considering students' assessment results, I constructed digital learning object quizzes to share with future students by embedding them in my institution's learning management system. For instance, I used Softchalk to license students' work using Creative Commons. Figure 5 contains an image of a Softchalk practice quiz I created from student questions. The Creative Commons license is visible in the bottom right-hand corner of the image.

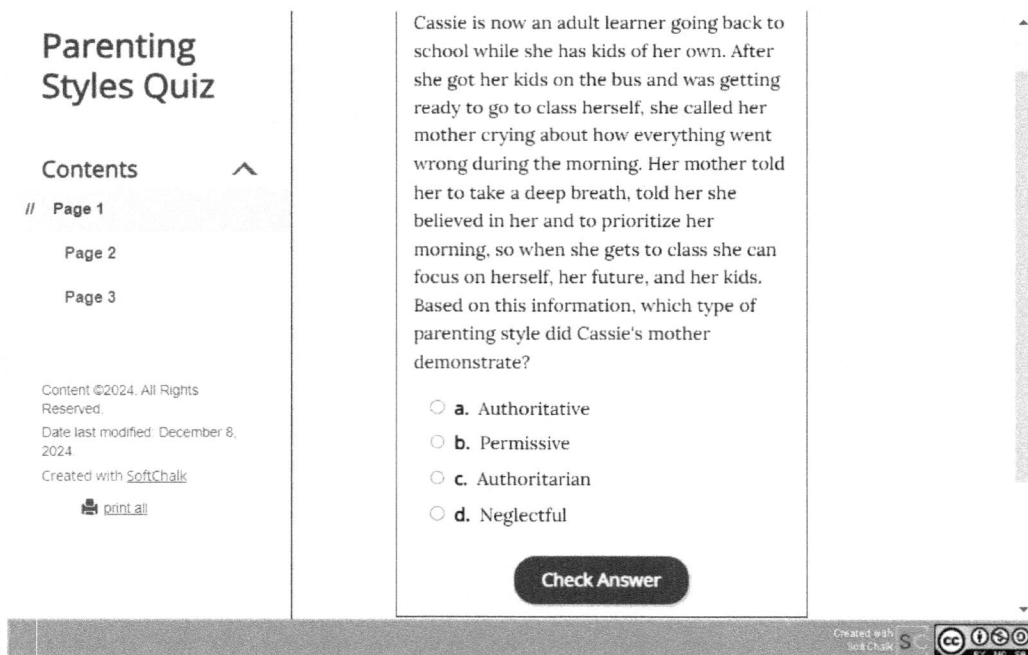

Figure 4: Image of Softchalk Quiz with Creative Common License

This assessment ends with discussing students' appraisals of bias and inclusive language in AI models. For a list of discussion questions, refer to Appendix D.

Debrief

I have utilized the AI multiple-choice assessment in two courses and intend to keep it a staple assessment in my curriculum. Students did a proficient job producing creative and unique questions representing our community. For instance, students noted the AI model's lack of the word "they/their" in question scenarios. Instead, AI uses specific male or female pronouns. Students also recalled the generative AI's lack of variety in name choices, such as Gemini's frequent use of Sarah, Emily, Sam, and Maya. The assessment, which increased student learning, exposed students to AI tools and inclusive principles, and added motivational value as a renewable assessment, urged students to demonstrate robust critical thinking skills.

Student survey results about the assessment were positive. Of the 31 student responses, only one indicated dissatisfaction with the AI-powered multiple-choice assessment concerning their learning. The remaining students reported being "very satisfied," "satisfied," or "neutral." This student sentiment aligns with the findings of Clinton-Lisell's (2021) meta-analysis that found students "generally perceived open pedagogy as positive and meaningful experiences" (p. 260). In another study by Clinton-Lisell and Gwozdz (2023), they further discovered that "students reported higher levels of intrinsic motivation (inherent interest and enjoyment) with renewable assignments than traditional assignments" (p. 131). Overall, students in my courses agreed with previous students and had a worthwhile, satisfying learning experience.

Even the most positive learning experiences come with some challenges, and executing this assessment also did. The assessment was initially designed for an upper-level Educational Psychology course but was later adapted for a lower-level Introduction to Psychology course. A key observation from the adaptation was that students in the introductory course showed less attention to assignment details than their upper-level counterparts. For example, some students only submitted one question instead of three. This could be due to the differences in student populations—Educational Psychology students are typically more focused, while Introduction to Psychology students come from various academic backgrounds and abilities.

Another assumption I made in the introductory course was that students would generate another question if the AI generated one didn't apply to our course content or was not a scenario-based question. Students did not take this initiative. To avoid future confusion, I updated the student directions (see Appendix A) to explain to students that they can generate multiple questions to evaluate and will emphasize the importance of generating scenario-based questions for revision.

When reflecting on the management of this project, I uncovered technological and time management challenges. The time to grade this assessment was manageable, and the grading rubric (see Appendix A) was efficient. While this assessment is not labor intensive to deploy or grade, collecting and selecting quality multiple-choice questions can be time consuming. This is a challenge reported by many instructors when constructing and deploying open pedagogical projects (Lazzara et al., 2024). In addition, I discovered that downloading PDF documents from the learning management system could be tedious, time consuming, and didn't provide a smooth transition to an exam question repository. I found that Google and Microsoft Forms survey tools allow respondents to upload documents and images while completing surveys. These tools could streamline student responses, integrate nuanced directions in real-time for students, and save time by pooling questions into one column in an Excel document.

Appraisal

While this assessment presented in this chapter is designed for introductory course students at a university or college, this summative assessment can be modified to enhance a course focusing on quality assessment construction, such as courses titled: Tests and Measurements, Educational Assessment and Measurement, Curriculum Design and Development, and Educational Psychology. The assessment directions and rubric specifications could be modified to focus more on effective question stem construction, and students could identify, write, and justify question distractors.

One of the limitations of this assessment is that students could use AI to write some of their ranking rationales. I have found that when asking AI to provide a ranking explanation of the incorrect answers to a multiple-choice question, the AI frequently lumps some of the incorrect answers together, limiting students' abilities to use LLMs to circumvent constructing their original rationales. Requiring students to use peer-reviewed course materials to write their explanations increases the likelihood and accountability of students utilizing their critical thinking to write their justifications.

Another limitation of this assessment is that it only applies to the generation of multiple-choice style questions due to the ranking of incorrect questions. Nevertheless, students could generate and revise short case studies using diverse perspectives and self-representation that could be used for extensive essay exam questions. When doing so, however, the cognitive benefits outlined in this chapter may differ.

Summary

This chapter explored a novel approach to incorporating generative AI into higher education assessment. By leveraging the capabilities of large language models, learners were tasked with creating and refining multiple-choice questions, cultivating critical thinking, and promoting diversity, equity, and inclusion. This chapter demonstrates that traditional assessment practices can be enhanced through AI integration, leading to more engaging and effective learning experiences. This assessment challenged students to evaluate and improve AI-generated content and empowered them to contribute to a growing repository of open educational resources.

The integration of AI into the classroom presents both opportunities and challenges. While AI can automate certain tasks and generate content, maintaining a human-centered approach to education is essential to ensure students use AI as a tool rather than a replacement for human ingenuity and critical thinking. As AI technology evolves, educators must adapt their pedagogical practices accordingly. By embracing innovative assessment strategies like the one presented in this chapter, instructors in higher education can prepare students for the challenges and opportunities of the 21st century.

References

American Psychological Association. (2023). *Inclusive language guide* (2nd ed.). https://www.apa.org/about/apa/ equity-diversity-inclusion/language-guidelines.pdf

Bowen, J. & Watson C. (2024). *Teaching with AI: A practical guide to a new era of human learning.* John Hopkins Press.

Churchill, D. (2007). Towards a useful classification of learning objects. *Educational Technology Research and Development, 55*(5), 479–497. https://doi.org/10.1007/s11423-006-9000-y

Clinton-Lisell, V. (2021). Open pedagogy: A systematic review of empirical findings. *Journal of Learning of Learning for Development, 8*(2), 255-268. https://files.eric.ed.gov/fulltext/ EJ1314199.pdf

Clinton-Lisell, V. & Gwozdz, L. (2023). Understanding student experiences of renewable and traditional assignments. *College Teaching, 71*(2), 125-134. https://doi.org/10.1080/ 87567555.2023.2179591

Harvard, B. (n.d.). Ranking multiple-choice answers to increase cognition. *The Effortful Educator.* https://theeffortfuleducator.com/2020/04/27/rmcatic/

Herder, L. (2023). AI: A brilliant but biased tool for education. *Diverse Issues in Higher Education, 40*(11), 20-22. https://research.ebsco.com/linkprocessor/plink?id=add7ade8-0d50-3f0f-b875-70719e4539b6

Jhangiani, R. (2017). Ditching the "Disposable assignment" in favor of open pedagogy.In W. Altman & L. Stein (Eds.), *Essays from Excellence in Teaching.* https://doi.org/10.31219/ osf.io/g4kfx

Lazzara, J., Bloom, M., & Clinton-Lisell, V. (2024). Renewable assignments: Comparing faculty and student perceptions. *Open Praxis, 16*(4), pp. 514–525. https://doi.org/10.55982/ openpraxis.16.4.706

Leffer, L. (2023, October 26). Humans absorb bias from AI—and keep it after they stop using the algorithm. *Scientific American.* https://www.scientificamerican.com/article/humans-absorb-bias-from-ai-and-keep-it-after-they-stop-using-the-algorithm/

Moshman, D. (1982). Exogenous, endogenous, and dialectical constructivism. *Developmental Review, 2*(4), 371-384. https://doi.org/10.1016/0273-2297(82)90019-3

Ng, D., Leung, J., Chu, S., & Qiao, M. (2021). Conceptualizing AI literacy: An exploratory review. *Computers and Education: Artificial Intelligence, 2*, 1-11. https://doi.org/10.1016/j.caeai.2021.100041

Roelle, J., Schweppe, J., Endres, T., Lachner, A., von Aufschnaiter, C., Renkl, A., Eitel, A., Leutner, D., Rummer, R., Scheiter, K., & Vorholzer, A. (2022). Combining retrieval practice and generative learning in educational contexts: Promises and challenges. *Open Science in Psychology, 54*(4), 142–150. https://doi.org/10.1026/0049-8637/a000261

Schunk, D. (2020). *Learning theories: An educational perspective* (8th ed.). Pearson.

Simpson, T. L. (2002). Dare I oppose constructivist theory? *The Educational Forum, 66*(4), 347–354. https://doi.org/10.1080/00131720208984854

Walter, Y. (2024). Embracing the future of artificial intelligence in the classroom: The relevance of AI literacy, prompt engineering, and critical thinking in modern education. *International Journal of Educational Technology in Higher Education, 21*, 1-29. https://doi.org/10.1186/s41239-024-00448-3

Wiley, D., & Hilton III, J. L. (2018). Defining OER-Enabled Pedagogy. *The International Review of Research in Open and Distributed Learning, 19*(4), 133-147.https://doi.org/10.19173/irrodl.v19i4.3601

Xia, Q., Weng, X., Ouyang, F., Lin, T., & Chiu, T. (2024). A scoping review on how generative artificial intelligence transforms assessment in higher education. *International Journal of Educational Technology in Higher Education, 21*(40), 1-22. https://doi.org/10.1186/s41239-024-00468-z

Zeide, E. (2019). Artificial intelligence in higher education: Applications, promise and perils, and ethical questions. *Educase Review.* https://er.educause.edu/articles/2019/8/artificial-intelligence-in-higher-education-applications-promise-and-perils-and-ethical-questions

Chapter 4 Appendices

Appendix A: Assignment Guidelines for the Artificial Intelligence Multiple-Choice Question Assessment

For the ease of assessment adoption, I have provided the assignment documentation that is provided directly to students. This appendix includes the assessment's learning objectives, description, directions for completion, and grading rubric for instructor use. Since this material is openly licensed, readers can retain, revise, remix, reuse or redistribute this documentation according to this book's open license specifications.

Learning Objectives

- Construct AI prompts to generate scenario-based multiple-choice questions based on course concepts and theories.
- Evaluate AI-constructed multiple-choice questions for accuracy, structure, and bias.
- Apply theoretical perspectives to hypothetical scenarios when revising AI responses.
- Apply accurate representations of diversity, equity, & inclusion principles through the revision of contextual details and language in questions.
- Justify the accuracy of the AI multiple choice questions utilizing critical thinking skills and peer-reviewed course materials.
- Write logical arguments to support the ranking of incorrect answers.

Assignment Description

For this assignment, you will utilize an artificially intelligent large language model such as ChatGPT or Google's Gemini to assist you in the construction of scenario-based multiple-choice questions on course concepts and theories. While large language models can write effective multiple-choice questions, they do a poor job of constructing specific questions that ask test takers to apply their knowledge to real-life scenarios. AI also struggles to use inclusive language that represents our multi-faceted, multicultural environment. Therefore, you will be tasked with evaluating, revising, and justifying AI questions for use by students in future classes. The questions will be openly licensed using SoftChalk and embedded in our learning management system for future students to use when studying for course exams.

Directions for Assignment Completion

1. First, you will want to write a "prompt" to type into the generative AI program (Google Gemini, ChatGPT, etc.). A prompt is "any form of text, question, information, or coding that communicates to AI what response you're looking for" (CoSchedule, 2024.). Depending on how you phrase your prompt, AI could provide varying responses.

2. Next, prompt the artificial intelligence (Google Gemini or ChatGPT) to construct one **scenario-based or problem-based** multiple-choice question based on <insert a course chapter or specific theories here>. Make sure to include in your prompt that the question should be **scenario-based**, includes the educational level of your future test takers (ie. undergraduate students), and that you want the AI to include the correct answer to the question in the results.

3. Take a screenshot of the prompt you generated and the AI's answer. If the terminology in the question is foreign to you, you can generate more than one question to ensure it matches our course materials. Paste the screenshot of your prompt and question into a Microsoft Word or Google document.

4. Next, you will need to investigate if the answer is correct using our peer-reviewed, current course materials (our textbook or lecture PowerPoints). Directly below the screenshot, include a short evaluation of the accuracy of ChatGPT or Gemini's answer to the question, including a ranking of the question's answers with your rationale for your ranking.

    a. If the answer AI provided is correct, you will need to identify where you found the correct answer to the question using your textbook. List the page and paragraph number where you found information that justifies why the answer is correct. Explain in a few short sentences why the answer is correct utilizing the information in your textbook.

    b. If you believe that the answer AI provided is incorrect, provide the page and paragraph number proving the answer is incorrect with an explanation of why it is incorrect utilizing the information in your textbook.

5. After confirming the accuracy of the answer, you will now review the question's remaining incorrect answer choices.

6. After you justify the accuracy of the question's answer, you will then rank the plausibility of the other answer's choices. You want to rank the remaining answer options from most correct to least correct. In a few sentences, explain why you ranked the answer choices in the manner that you did.

7. Next, it is time for the fun part! You are now going to revise the problem-based scenario to be more specific by adding context and details to the scenario. For instance, adding biographical information, such as names and ages, provides more context for your reader to answer the question. You should use inclusive names and language in

your revision. Your question scenario can be **NO longer than four sentences** and the details should remain significant to the question. The details should not distract or mislead the reader.

8. Review the answers to the question and make necessary adjustments where needed. All of the answer choices should be plausible, but only one should be the correct answer. Answers should also be written using a similar pattern of wording.

9. Finally, you will need to complete this process for three questions. A sample is provided on our learning management system for your review (Appendix B). Please format your document in the same order and with the same headers.

AI Multiple-Choice Assignment Grading Rubric

Criteria	Exceptional (100-90%)	Above Average/Average (89-70%)	Below Expectations (69-0%)
AI Prompt & Response (5%)	Submission included screenshots of the original artificial intelligence prompts and responses for all 3 questions.	Submission included screenshots of the original artificial intelligence prompts and responses for at least 2-1 questions.	Submission failed to include any screenshots of the artificial intelligence prompts and responses.
Rationale & Ranking (25%)	Demonstrated exceptional critical thinking when justifying the accuracy of the answers to the questions. Accurately ranked answer choices. Provided an exceptional ranking and explanation of the plausibility of the incorrect answer choices.	Demonstrated critical thinking when attempting to justify the accuracy of the answers to the questions. Most answer choices were ranked correctly. Provided a ranking and explanation of the plausibility of the incorrect answer choices. The explanations were unclear or needed additional specificity.	Lacked a clear demonstration of effective critical thinking skills when justifying answer accuracy and ranking answer choices.
Question Reconstruction (25%)	Demonstrated exceptional analytical and critical thinking through the revision of scenario-based multiple-choice questions. Added rich details without confusing student exam responders. Questions were adequately difficult for college students. All questions were no longer than 4 sentences in length.	Demonstrated analytical and critical thinking through the revision of scenario-based multiple-choice questions. Added details, yet had too many details or details confused student exam responder. Some questions were too easy or too difficult for college students. Some questions were longer than 4 sentences in length.	Lacked a clear demonstration of effective analytical and critical thinking skills in the revision of scenario-based multiple-choice questions. Most questions were too easy or too difficult for college students. All sentences were longer than 4 sentences in length.

Criteria	Exceptional (100-90%)	Above Average/Average (89-70%)	Below Expectations (69-0%)
Connection to Course Materials (15%)	Each answer and ranking rationale is tied to course materials with the inclusion of a page and paragraph number.	Most answer and ranking rationales are tied to course materials with the inclusion of page and paragraph numbers.	Answer and ranking rationales were not tied to course materials and lacked the inclusion of page and paragraph numbers.
Application of Diversity, Equity & Inclusion (25%)	Implements diverse and inclusive language in question scenarios. Names and details in scenarios represented a diverse population.	Attempts to implement diverse or inclusive language in question scenarios. Some names and details in scenarios represented a diverse population.	Lacks inclusive language in question scenarios and contains bias. Didn't demonstrate any diversity.

References

CoSchedule. (2024). AI prompt. *The Ultimate Marketing Dictionary of Terms and Definitions*. https://coschedule.com/marketing-terms-definitions

Appendix B: Sample of a Completed Student Assignment

The following is a completed student sample that I provide for students with the assignment directions and the corresponding grading rubric. Figure 1 is an image of a student written prompt entered into Google's Gemini AI generator. The image also includes the Google Gemini's response, which is a short multiple-choice question.

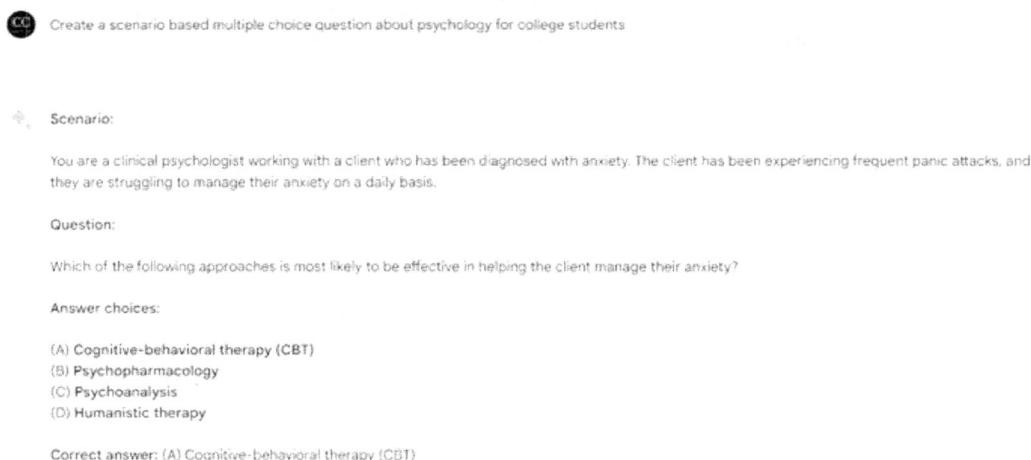

Create a scenario based multiple choice question about psychology for college students

Scenario:

You are a clinical psychologist working with a client who has been diagnosed with anxiety. The client has been experiencing frequent panic attacks, and they are struggling to manage their anxiety on a daily basis.

Question:

Which of the following approaches is most likely to be effective in helping the client manage their anxiety?

Answer choices:

(A) Cognitive-behavioral therapy (CBT)
(B) Psychopharmacology
(C) Psychoanalysis
(D) Humanistic therapy

Correct answer: (A) Cognitive-behavioral therapy (CBT)

Figure 1: Image of AI Generated Question Prior to Student Revision

Correct Answer Rationale

The correct answer is "Cognitive Behavioral Therapy" because CBT is a type of therapy that is effective in treating a wide range of psychological disorders, including anxiety. CBT focuses on identifying and changing negative thoughts and behaviors that contribute to the client's anxiety. The other answer choices are also valid approaches to treating anxiety, but they are not typically as effective as CBT for first-line treatment and our textbook advises CBT as the best approach (Course textbook, page 120, paragraphs 3-5).

Ranking Rationale

The next plausible answer to this question would be psychoanalysis. This would be less likely to be as effective or efficient as CBT for a specific anxiety disorder like generalized anxiety disorder. Psychoanalysis is a long-term therapy that focuses on exploring unconscious conflicts, which might be less relevant to Bill's immediate needs (Course textbook, page 125, paragraph 2).

The third option, humanistic theory, is much less likely to help Bill with his anxiety disorder since this approach focuses on personal growth and self-actualization, which might not directly address Bill's specific symptoms of anxiety and panic attacks. This may help Bill grow as a person, but his panic attacks are likely to remain (Course textbook, page 130, paragraph 4).

The least correct answer for this question is letter B or psychopharmacology because it states in the question scenario that Bill can't take SSRIs. Since we do not know more about Bill's health, we can't assume or eliminate the possibility that he could take a benzodiazepine. If he could take a benzodiazepine, it is recommended that he not take it for more than 2-4 weeks as it can cause physical dependence. Finally, our textbook author argues that benzodiazepines have been less effective in producing long-term change and CBT appears more effective for producing long-term change (Course textbook, page 135, paragraph 2).

Revised Question

Cara is a clinical psychologist working with a client named Amir who has been diagnosed with generalized anxiety disorder. Amir has been experiencing frequent panic attacks when praying at his local mosque and is struggling to manage their anxiety daily. Although Amir believes in taking medication for illnesses, he can't take anti-anxiety drugs (SSRIs) because they interfere with the Warfarin medication he is currently taking.

Which of the following approaches should Cara utilize to help Amir manage his anxiety effectively?

Answer choices:

A. Cognitive-behavioral therapy (CBT)
B. Psychopharmacology
C. Psychoanalysis
D. Humanistic Theory

Correct answer:

A. Cognitive-behavioral therapy (CBT)

Appendix C: Sample of Student Survey

The following is a list of the questions I gave students in a Google Form survey to collect and organize student preferences for sharing their work.

Questions	Response Formats
List your first and last name.	Short Answer
May I use your questions for future students? Some questions may be integrated into online digital quizzes that the public can access. Choose yes or no.	Multiple Choice
If your questions are used in a public online quiz, do you want me to include your name, or do you want to remain anonymous?	Multiple Choice Options include: • Please include my name to represent my work. • I am fine sharing the questions, but leave my name off the quiz. • I do not want to share my questions.

Students were also asked the following questions to assess the strengths and weaknesses of the assessment. The students' survey responses are discussed in the chapter's debrief section, and assessment revisions were made based on their feedback.

Questions	Response Formats
Did you find the process of revising and improving the AI-generated questions to be challenging?	Multiple Choice Options include: • Very challenging • Somewhat challenging • Neither challenging nor easy • Somewhat easy • Easy

Questions	Response Formats
How did you feel about sharing your revised questions for the benefit of future students?	Multiple Choice Options include: • Excited to contribute to future learning • Satisfied to be part of the process • Neutral • Slightly hesitant • Not interested in sharing
What were the biggest challenges you faced while completing the assessment?	Long-answer text

Appendix D: Discussion Questions: Reflecting on the AI-Generated Exam Question Assessment

Below is a list of potential student discussion questions:

1. What steps did you take to critically evaluate the AI-generated questions?
2. Based on the AI model's responses to your prompts, did you identify any bias? Can you provide an example?
3. How can humans ensure that AI-generated questions are culturally sensitive and inclusive? What strategies can be used to avoid bias and stereotypes?
4. How did you improve the quality of the AI-generated questions? What specific changes did you make to your questions to represent your life or the lives of others?
5. In your future career, how can you ensure your work is diverse and inclusive? What strategies can you use to avoid bias and stereotypes in your future career?

5. Partnering for Open Pedagogical Practices: Librarian Support in Campus Initiatives

Christina R. Hilburger, MISt

Chapter Learning Objectives:

- Examine how open pedagogy fosters inclusive, student-centered learning supported by librarian expertise.
- Identify strategies librarians can employ to guide faculty adoption of open pedagogy.
- Evaluate campus-wide models for sustaining open pedagogy, emphasizing librarians' contributions.
- Explore how librarians address institutional barriers to implementing open pedagogy.

Chapter Overview

This chapter explores how librarians at The State University of New York (SUNY) at Fredonia support open pedagogy. Originally aimed at reducing the cost of course materials, the initiative now empowers students as co-creators of knowledge. Librarians sustain open pedagogy efforts by partnering with faculty and students and securing administrative support. Fredonia's experiences offer insights into addressing barriers, engaging faculty, and fostering sustainable, innovative educational practices.

1. How can librarians and institutions collaboratively support faculty in adopting or designing open pedagogy endeavors?
2. What strategies can strengthen the alignment between faculty needs and institutional resources to support open pedagogy?
3. How can campuses sustain engagement in open pedagogy initiatives?

Rationale

In 2022, Open Fredonia was launched as a collaborative initiative co-led by Dawn Eckenrode, Director of the Professional Development Center, and me, representing the Daniel A. Reed Library. Building on Fredonia's earlier Open Education Resources (OER) initiatives aimed at cost reduction, Open Fredonia broadened its foundation by prioritizing open pedagogy as a transformative model. Early OER efforts saved students over $200,000 by developing 21 OER-based courses, reflecting Fredonia's commitment to accessibility and affordability (RPK Group, 2019). The shift to open pedagogy represented an expansion of Fredonia's foundational work with OER, prompted by the end of New York State's OER funding and the disruptions of the COVID-19 pandemic, addressing faculty needs while fostering inclusive and innovative teaching practices.

Open Educational Practices (OEP) and open pedagogy transform traditional teaching into inclusive, collaborative models. As Maultsaid and Harrison (2023) discuss, these approaches promote shared accountability and mutual respect, empowering students as co-creators of knowledge. These approaches replace 'disposable assignments,' which hold no lasting value, with 'renewable assignments' that create meaningful, reusable resources for the academic community and beyond (Bloom, 2019, pp. 343–345). This shift highlights the potential of open pedagogy to foster deeper engagement by encouraging students to contribute lasting work that benefits both their peers and wider audiences.

OEP and open pedagogy transform traditional, instructor-led teaching into participatory and collaborative models centered on student engagement and empowerment, although practical barriers such as time constraints and lack of institutional support often discourage adoption (Paskevicius & Irvine, 2019, pp. 24–26; Wiley & Hilton, 2018). Bloom (2019) emphasizes the potential of renewable assignments to engage students meaningfully without compromising learning outcomes. Grounded in theoretical frameworks such as Vygotsky's social constructivism (Vygotsky, 1978) and Freire's pedagogy of empowerment (Freire, 1970), these approaches emphasize the value of collaborative, student-driven learning. These approaches empower students as co-creators of knowledge, fostering engagement, inclusivity, and accessibility (Chen & Hendricks, 2023).

For instance, in a criminal justice seminar, I worked with students who co-authored *Perspectives on Incarceration*, an OER text exploring topics like the pains of imprisonment and cultural portrayals of incarceration. Similarly, animation students developed a toolkit for aspiring artists, blending creative practice with community engagement. These projects exemplify how collaboration amplifies the reach and impact of open pedagogy, a concept echoed by Katz (2019), who highlights the critical role of librarians in fostering partnerships that align institutional goals with innovative, student-centered educational practices (pp. 382-384).

Fredonia's approach aligns with its institutional priorities of accessibility, inclusivity, and affordability (The State University of New York at Fredonia, 2023). By integrating theoretical frameworks like Vygotsky's social constructivism and Freire's pedagogy of empowerment alongside strategic librarian support, Fredonia exemplifies how institutions can effectively implement and sustain open pedagogy initiatives. Librarians have been central to this transition, leveraging their expertise to guide OER integration, address systemic challenges like copyright complexities, and advocate for sustainable practices. These efforts show how strategic partnerships amplify open pedagogy's impact.

Masterman (2016) identifies structural challenges for fostering OEP, including decentralized governance and faculty autonomy, which often hinder coordinated adoption efforts. In particular, research-intensive institutions face unique barriers, such as entrenched norms and a lack of clear policies supporting open education (Masterman, 2016). These observations reflect Fredonia's experience, where librarians actively addressed systemic challenges through strategic collaboration and advocacy to promote institutional alignment. Fredonia's emphasis on student co-authorship and collaborative knowledge creation reflects the broader goals of open pedagogy to make learning inclusive and participatory.

As noted by Chen & Hendricks (2023), open pedagogy assignments increase student engagement and motivate higher-quality work, emphasizing the value of renewable assignments as a tool for inclusive and participatory learning. Tualaulelei and Green (2023) highlight the fragmented nature of professional learning opportunities for equity-focused pedagogy and advocate for integrating structured OEP to empower students. This approach aligns with Freire's vision by valuing students' unique perspectives and experiences, fostering inclusivity and active engagement.

This chapter explores the theoretical foundations of open pedagogy and its alignment with equity-focused goals, thus highlighting librarians' roles in advancing OEP through professional development and collaboration. It outlines strategies for fostering inclusive, student-centered learning grounded in trust, attentiveness, and shared accountability, as emphasized by Maultsaid and Harrison (2023). These relational practices align with Freire's and Vygotsky's participatory, student-driven education theories. By integrating these principles, Fredonia reinforces its commitment to equity and equips students with skills for creating and sharing knowledge.

Librarians' Roles in Advancing OEP and Open Pedagogy at Fredonia

SUNY Fredonia's librarians play a critical role in advancing Open Educational Practices (OEP) by providing professional development, fostering collaboration, and advocating for institutional support. Their contributions ensure faculty and students are empowered to adopt innovative teaching and learning practices. Moreover, their multifaceted efforts, from guiding open pedagogy project planning to promoting strategic initiatives, create a robust foundation for innovative teaching and learning practices.

Professional Development and Collaboration

My librarian colleagues and I promote development and collaboration by leading workshops and one-on-one consultations and offering Discovery Labs to support faculty adopting OER and integrating open pedagogy into their courses. These initiatives focus on equipping faculty with practical skills, such as identifying OER, navigating Creative Commons licensing and accessibility requirements, and designing collaborative assignments aligned with open pedagogy principles. Financial incentives, such as stipends for course redesigns, further encourage faculty participation, with librarians providing tailored guidance. As Wesolek et al. (2018) emphasize, librarians are uniquely positioned to guide faculty through licensing complexities and resource curation. Okamoto (2013) highlights how these efforts reduce textbook costs and also promote accessibility and equity. By cultivating these outcomes, librarians align their support with institutional priorities, strengthening the impact and sustainability of OER initiatives.

Promoting collaboration between librarians and faculty is fundamental to advancing sustainable open educational practices (Borchard & Magnuson, 2017). Borchard and Magnuson (2017) also highlight that librarians play a pivotal role in engaging faculty through tailored workshops and individualized consultations. Librarians can bridge gaps between institutional priorities and faculty goals by demonstrating the impact of affordable learning initiatives, such as cost savings and enhanced student engagement. Fredonia's Discovery Labs is a practical example of developing trust and facilitating co-creating strategies tailored to course objectives. Informal exchanges, as described by Gilpin, et al. (2023), help build trust and motivate faculty to experiment with open pedagogy. Fredonia's Discovery Labs serve as an example of this collaborative and informal environment fostering innovation.

Librarians advocate for administrative support to sustain OEP initiatives. After New York State OER funding ended in 2020 (SUNY OER Services, n.d.), we worked with Fredonia's administration to secure internal funding for course redesigns and faculty stipends.

Additionally, librarians lead grant writing efforts to obtain external funding, broadening the focus from reducing textbook costs to supporting open pedagogy and student engagement. Okamoto (2013) emphasizes the importance of integrating OER initiatives into institutional frameworks to ensure sustainability. By aligning project milestones with campus-wide objectives and providing faculty incentives, institutions can promote both participation and longevity. McNally and Santiago (2023) highlight the need for institutional alignment to sustain librarian-led open pedagogy initiatives. Our strategic approach to sustaining OER initiatives at Fredonia has involved advocating for librarian contributions and aligning funding priorities with institutional goals. These efforts highlight librarians' strategic role in aligning institutional priorities with faculty and student needs, ensuring the long-term impact of OEP.

Open Pedagogy Project Planning

A comprehensive support framework is essential for integrating collaborative, student-centered learning into higher education. This framework connects institutional resources, faculty development, and student engagement to the goals of open pedagogy. By aligning these elements, institutions can manage the complexities of implementing innovative teaching approaches, such as ensuring technological infrastructure or encouraging faculty and student buy-in.

From 2021 to 2022, I participated in the SPARC Open Education Leadership Program, a professional development experience that prepared me to co-lead open education initiatives at Fredonia. As part of my capstone project, I developed Open Fredonia, a new open education program at my institution that expanded beyond OER adoption to include more comprehensive applications of open education. To support this effort, I developed the *Building Upon an Established OER Initiative Toolkit* to help institutions evaluate readiness and set goals for open pedagogy adoption. The toolkit is designed to help institutions assess their readiness to adopt open pedagogy, set realistic goals, and engage stakeholders effectively.

As an additional resource, other campuses' open education leaders can use the Campus Readiness Gauge, illustrated in Figure 1, to evaluate their college or university's institutional readiness for open pedagogy.

An interactive H5P element has been excluded from this version of the text. You can view it online here:

https://milnepublishing.geneseo.edu/emphasizing-a-student-centered-process/?p=32#h5p-1

Figure 1: Campus Readiness Gauge

This diagnostic tool provides a structured way to assess alignment across six key areas, identifying gaps and areas for improvement. Masterman (2016) notes that research-intensive institutions often lack the policies and cultural acceptance needed to scale OEP. In my experience, using this assessment helps strategically allocate resources and prioritize readiness initiatives, setting the stage for sustainable open pedagogy efforts.

Addressing these barriers helps institutions create the conditions for sustained progress in open education. For example, Tualaulelei and Green (2023) emphasize that equity-focused professional development can address the challenges of fragmented support systems by helping institutions nurture a culture of collaboration and innovation through structured OEP initiatives. This alignment ensures that faculty development efforts are effective and grounded in broader institutional priorities for inclusivity.

I found that structured assessments like these equip institutions to support faculty and students effectively, setting the stage for successful open pedagogy initiatives. McNally and Santiago (2023) argue that sustaining open pedagogy initiatives requires embedding milestone planning within broader institutional frameworks (McNally & Santiago, 2023). Table 1 outlines key milestones for institutions to guide planning, from engaging participants to providing ongoing support during course delivery. As Gilpin, et al. (2023) emphasize, celebrating milestones reinforces faculty and student engagement to create a culture of openness and innovation.

Table 1: *Using the Campus Readiness Gauge to Evaluate Open Pedagogy Capacity*

Component	Description	Key Questions to Assess Readiness
Infrastructure	The technological and logistical foundation necessary to support open pedagogy, including digital tools, and platforms.	• Does the institution have the digital tools and platforms to implement open pedagogy projects? • Are there systems in place to manage and distribute OER?
Resources	Financial, personnel, and material resources are available to support faculty in adopting open pedagogy.	• Are there financial incentives or grants available for faculty? • Is there dedicated staff (e.g., instructional designers, librarians) to support faculty?
Policies	Institutional policies that encourage or mandate the adoption of open educational practices.	• Are there clear policies supporting open pedagogy at the institutional level? • Do policies allow faculty freedom to use and create open resources?
Faculty Engagement	The level of interest, participation, and commitment from faculty in implementing open pedagogy.	• Are faculty engaged and motivated to adopt open pedagogy? • Is there a community of practice where faculty can share experiences and resources?
Student Support	Availability of academic and technological support for students engaging in open pedagogy projects.	• Do students have access to the resources for open pedagogy, such as the know-how to find and access OER and/or digital tools? • Is there support for students to engage in knowledge co-creation?

Component	Description	Key Questions to Assess Readiness
Cultural Readiness	The overall institutional culture's openness to innovation, collaboration, and change.	• Is there a culture of innovation and collaboration at the institution? • Are administrators, faculty, and students open to new pedagogical models?

These assessments ensure institutions are prepared to support faculty and students effectively, setting the stage for successful open pedagogy initiatives. Table 2 outlines key milestones for institutions to guide planning, from engaging participants to providing ongoing support during course delivery.

Table 2: *Key Milestones for Open Pedagogy Project Planning*

Timeframe	Description	Milestone
6-12 months prior	Identify Participants	Engage faculty who will participate in open pedagogy projects and create interest and awareness. Initial Training Sessions: Conduct workshops to familiarize faculty with open pedagogy principles and practices.
6-10 months prior	Project Planning	Confirm which courses and sections will include open pedagogy and establish project goals.
4-6 months prior	Design and Content Development	Work with faculty to develop course materials and plan how students will be engaged as co-creators.
3-6 weeks prior	Finalize Course Set-up	Ensure all course content and collaborative tools are integrated and ready for use.
2-4 weeks prior	Launch and Monitor	Begin courses and provide ongoing support as faculty implement open pedagogy in their teaching.

Paskevicius and Irvine (2019) emphasize aligning project milestones with institutional resources to overcome barriers, while collaborative spaces and clear benchmarks promote innovation and steady advancement. Effective project management is crucial for implementing open pedagogy initiatives successfully. Regular check-ins with faculty and support teams ensure consistent progress while providing opportunities to address emerging challenges. For example, these meetings can serve as a platform to troubleshoot issues and refine strategies, thus keeping all participants aligned on project goals. Setting clear measures enables faculty to understand a project's milestones and maintain focus on objectives, which provides a sense of direction and accountability. Sharing effective practices such as this stimulates a collaborative environment where faculty and librarians can exchange ideas and strategies. This, in turn, enhances the overall quality of the initiative. Proactively addressing common barriers—such as technical issues or time constraints—also helps maintain momentum and prevents stagnation during implementation. Finally, celebrating achievements, such as reaching milestones or completing successful projects, reinforces engagement and cultivates a positive culture around open pedagogy. By incorporating these strategies, institutions can help ensure that open pedagogy projects are well-supported and sustainable.

Supporting Faculty Efforts to Integrate OER in Curriculum

Due to limited awareness, time constraints, and concerns about resource quality, faculty often need help integrating OER into their teaching. Faculty surveys can also be a valuable tool for identifying and addressing these barriers (Braddlee & VanScoy, 2019). A survey instrument included in Appendix A provides a structured approach to understanding faculty needs, challenges, and opportunities for supporting OER adoption. Braddlee and VanScoy (2019) also highlight that librarians are uniquely positioned to bridge the gap between faculty's pedagogical goals and institutional support structures, offering both technical expertise and advocacy to reduce barriers to OER adoption. At Fredonia, librarians provide individualized consultations and workshops, simplifying the complexities of OER adoption while aligning resources with course objectives. These strategies empower faculty to embrace open pedagogy and contribute to a campus culture of innovation.

Technical and licensing issues can further complicate OER adoption (Paskevicius & Irvine, 2019), especially for faculty unfamiliar with Creative Commons or digital tools (Wiley & Hilton, 2018). Cronin et al. (2023) highlight systemic barriers to OER adoption, such as faculty time constraints and limited institutional support. These barriers can discourage even motivated educators from exploring OER as a teaching option. Librarians are uniquely positioned to mitigate these challenges by providing targeted support, such as training on OER tools and institutional alignment. To address these challenges, librarians at Fredonia use targeted strategies that empower faculty and promote sustainable practices. This experience illustrates actionable strategies other librarians can adopt to advance open pedagogy initiatives at their institutions. Actional strategies for institutions could include:

- Professional Development: Librarian-led workshops provide practical training on finding, evaluating, and adapting OER.
- Customized Course Support: One-on-one consultations help faculty align OER with course objectives and troubleshoot challenges during adoption.

Recognition and Incentives: While formal recognition of OER contributions in tenure and promotion guidelines remains inconsistent across departments, initiatives at Fredonia have significantly increased awareness of the value of OER among faculty. Werth and Williams (2023) argue that recognizing OER contributions in tenure and promotion guidelines motivates faculty and validates the value of their work, a model that SUNY supports broadly. I found that offering stipends for course redesigns and including OER-related contributions in tenure and promotion guidelines motivates faculty participation.

Fostering a Community of Practice: Informal gatherings and peer-led discussions create a collaborative environment where faculty can share experiences, learn from each other, and build confidence in adopting OER. These efforts have significantly increased faculty engagement with OER, fostering a culture of openness and collaboration at Fredonia.

Supporting Faculty Efforts to Integrate Open Pedagogy in Curriculum

Faculty often encounter unique challenges when integrating open pedagogy into their teaching, even if they are familiar with OER. Bloom (2019) notes that resistance can stem from the complexity of implementing student-centered practices, highlighting the need for scaffolding and providing clear examples. These measures ensure both faculty and students feel confident navigating open pedagogy assignments. Unlike OER, which focuses on resource accessibility, open pedagogy emphasizes student-centered practices where learners actively contribute to course content.

Faculty may be hesitant to adopt these models due to concerns about their complexity, time constraints, or uncertainty about student preparedness. To overcome these barriers, librarians at Fredonia provide targeted support that empowers faculty to experiment with and embrace open pedagogy. By adopting these strategies, librarians can help faculty overcome hesitations, facilitate student-centered practices, and reinforce institutional commitments to inclusivity, equity, and innovative teaching. These approaches address immediate challenges and contribute to a sustainable culture of collaboration and engagement, positioning open pedagogy as a transformative educational model. Specific strategies include:

- Building Faculty Confidence through Workshops and Examples: Librarians offer workshops featuring case studies, templates, and rubrics to clarify open pedagogy principles. These sessions demonstrate how assignments can promote student agency and public engagement, reducing faculty concerns about implementation complexity.
- Mentorship and Peer Networks: Establishing mentorship programs and peer communities allows experienced faculty to guide colleagues, fostering shared learning and dialogue (Maultsaid & Harrison, 2023).
- Collaborative Assignment Design: Librarians collaborate with faculty to co-create open pedagogy assignments that align with course objectives. This includes troubleshooting, pedagogical guidance, and examples of successful projects, such as co-authored textbooks or community toolkits.
- Demonstrating the Value of Open Pedagogy: Highlighting the benefits—enhanced student engagement, inclusivity, and real-world skill development—helps faculty see the value of adopting these practices for themselves and their students (Paskevicius & Irvine, 2019).

- By addressing faculty concerns through targeted support, Fredonia's librarians have successfully facilitated the integration of open pedagogy into college and university curricula. Workshops, mentorship programs, collaborative assignment design, and emphasis on the tangible benefits of open pedagogy empower faculty to overcome challenges and adopt innovative teaching practices. These efforts enhance student engagement and inclusivity and contribute to a campus culture that values cooperation, creativity, and equitable education. As faculty grow more confident in implementing open pedagogy, their work reinforces Fredonia's broader institutional priorities of accessibility, innovation, and student-centered learning, creating a lasting impact on the academic community.

Supporting Students' Efforts to Create OER and Contribute to Open Pedagogy

Students are critical partners in open pedagogy, with librarians uniquely positioned to support their engagement and overcome challenges such as limited awareness or technical barriers. Many students lack awareness of what OER entails or feel unsure about their ability to contribute meaningful content (Chen & Hendricks, 2023). Additionally, as Chen & Hendricks (2023) highlight, the public visibility of student work in open pedagogy assignments can contribute to heightened stress and time management challenges, underscoring the need for scaffolded support. Technical and accessibility barriers and anxiety about public-facing work can also hinder student participation (Paskevicius & Irvine, 2019). To empower students and encourage meaningful engagement, librarians and instructors at Fredonia implement strategies that readers can adapt to support their student-centered initiatives. These include:

- Scaffolded Assignments and Clear Guidelines: Breaking down OER creation into manageable steps ensures students build their skills incrementally.
- Co-hosting Skill-Building Workshops: Early in the term, librarians and faculty host workshops on copyright, licensing, and effective digital communication. These sessions help students understand their rights as creators and prepare them to contribute high-quality work to OER projects (Gilpin et al., 2023).
- Celebrating Student Contributions: Highlighting student-created OER through campus events, digital repositories, or class presentations advances a sense of accomplishment and encourages participation. For example, Fredonia students who co-authored an open textbook showcased their work at a library-hosted event.
- Providing Accessible Tools and Resources: User-friendly platforms and equitable access to digital tools are critical for student success. Librarians provide hands-on guidance to bridge technical gaps and ensure students have the resources to engage fully (Cronin et

al., 2023).

- Building a Supportive Environment: A supportive classroom culture prioritizes collaboration and allows students to take risks without fear of failure. Librarians and instructors play a pivotal role by offering constructive feedback, reinforcing the importance of creativity, and encouraging shared ownership of educational outcomes.

Supporting students in creating OER and participating in open pedagogy projects enhances their learning experience and prepares them to be active contributors in a knowledge-driven society. Fredonia's approach offers a model for motivating students' engagement through scaffolded assignments and skill-building workshops that reduce technical and emotional barriers. Celebrating student contributions and providing accessible tools further empower learners, showing them the value of their work in real-world contexts. These strategies emphasize the importance of aligning institutional support with student needs to create an inclusive, participatory academic culture. By adopting similar approaches, librarians and educators can inspire students to become knowledge co-creators, helping democratize education and promote equity through collaborative learning practices.

Debrief

Fredonia's efforts to implement open pedagogy align with broader trends in higher education. Institutions are grappling with funding challenges, evolving pedagogical models, and increasing demands for equity and accessibility. To sustain and scale innovative practices, these initiatives require strategic planning, collaboration, and continuous evaluation. Drawing from Fredonia's experience, the following actionable strategies offer a roadmap for institutions seeking to adopt and expand open pedagogy initiatives. These strategies include:

- Build Interdisciplinary Teams: Collaboration across disciplines strengthens open pedagogy initiatives by integrating diverse perspectives and pooling expertise. At Fredonia, interdisciplinary teams—including librarians, faculty, instructional designers, and administrators—work together to address challenges holistically. These collaborations have led to the development of co-authored textbooks and community toolkits, engaging students in meaningful, real-world applications of their learning.
- Strategically Improve Participation: Addressing specific barriers—such as faculty time constraints or perceived resource quality—can encourage broader participation in open pedagogy. Fredonia has effectively used financial incentives, professional development workshops, and peer-led discussions to engage faculty. Highlighting early adopters' successes, such as faculty who redesigned courses or collaborated on impactful OER projects, further motivates others to explore open pedagogy.
- Foster a Culture of Openness: Promoting openness, inclusivity, and collaboration helps

integrate open pedagogy into the campus culture. Fredonia showcases the outcomes of its open pedagogy initiatives through its Open Fredonia website, which features co-authored textbooks, student projects like the COMM102 Wiki, and pages spotlighting faculty achievements.

- Measure Impact Through Surveys and Feedback: Evaluating the effectiveness of open pedagogy initiatives is essential for sustaining momentum. Faculty surveys can assess awareness, challenges, and satisfaction with available support, while student feedback provides insights into engagement and learning outcomes (Paskevicius & Irvine, 2019).

In sum, as Fredonia's experience demonstrates, librarians support students in mastering research, drafting, and peer review by providing clear guidance that makes each step of the process accessible and manageable. Strategic collaboration, intentional support, and rigorous evaluation are key to cultivating learning environments that advance accessibility, equity, and academic excellence. By leveraging librarians' expertise and fostering interdisciplinary connections, campuses can address systemic barriers and create transformative educational experiences that resonate with students' diverse and evolving needs.

Summary

Fredonia's open pedagogy initiatives have cultivated a culture of collaboration, inclusivity, and student-centered learning driven by interdisciplinary partnerships among librarians, faculty, instructional designers, and administrators. Librarians play a pivotal role by curating resources, leading professional development, and co-developing innovative OER materials like co-authored textbooks and community toolkits that engage students in real-world applications of learning. However, these efforts face challenges, including precarious library funding and the need for systematic evaluation. Moving forward, Fredonia plans to build on its successes by enhancing faculty support through targeted mentorship programs and simplifying OER adoption's technical aspects to lower participation barriers. The university also intends to deepen its focus on equity by integrating culturally responsive materials into OER offerings and expanding initiatives that celebrate diverse student voices. Addressing these challenges while maintaining a strong commitment to library resources and expanding evaluation frameworks will ensure the sustainability and growth of Fredonia's open pedagogy initiatives, fostering a more inclusive, innovative academic environment for all.

References

Bloom, M. (2019). Assessing the impact of "open pedagogy" on student skills mastery in first-year composition. *Open Praxis, 11*(4), 343-353. https://doi.org/ggzfkb

Borchard, L., & Magnuson, L. (2017). Library leadership in open educational resource adoption and affordable learning initiatives. *Urban Library Journal, 23*(1), 1-12. https://academic-works.cuny.edu/ulj

Braddlee, D., & VanScoy, A. (2019). Bridging the chasm: Faculty support roles for academic librarians in the adoption of open educational resources. *College & Research Libraries, 80*(4), 426-449. https://doi.org/nv5d

Chen, D., & Hendricks, C. (2023). Open pedagogy benefits and challenges: Student perceptions of writing open case studies. *Open Praxis, 15*(1), 27-36. https://doi.org/nv5f

Cronin, C., Havemann, L., Karunanayaka, S., & McAvinia, C. (2023). Open educational practices. *EdTechnica: The Open Encyclopedia of Educational Technology*, 147-153. https://doi.org/nv5g

Freire, P. (1970). *Pedagogy of the oppressed*. Continuum.

Gilpin, S. A., Rollag Yoon, S., & Lazzara, J. (2023). Building open pedagogy in community colleges. *Online Learning, 27*(4). https://doi.org/nv5h

Katz, S. (2019). Leveraging library expertise in support of institutional goals: A case study of an open educational resources initiative. *New Review of Academic Librarianship, 25*(4), 381-391. https://doi.org/nv5j

Masterman, E. (2016). Bringing open educational practice to a research-intensive university: Prospects and challenges. *The Electronic Journal of e-Learning, 14*(1). https://eric.ed.gov/?id=EJ1099364

Maultsaid, D., & Harrison, M. (2023). Can open pedagogy encourage care? Student perspectives. *The International Review of Research in Open and Distributed Learning, 24*(3), 77–98. https://doi.org/nv5k

Okamoto, K. (2013). Making higher education more affordable, one course reading at a time: Academic libraries as key advocates for open access textbooks and educational resources. *Public Services Quarterly, 9*(4), 267-283. https://doi.org/gf645x

Paskevicius, M., & Irvine, V. (2019). Practicalities of implementing open pedagogy in higher education. *Smart Learning Environments, 6*(1), 23. https://doi.org/ggfngv

McNally C., K., & Santiago, A. (2023). Exploring sustainability in library support for open pedagogy collaborations. *Communications in Information Literacy, 17*(1). https://doi.org/nv5m

RPK Group. (2019). *OER sustainability case study: SUNY Fredonia*. https://bit.ly/3OKhqj8

SUNY OER Services. (n.d.). *Projects and grants*. The State University of New York. https://bit.ly/49ucVCD

The State University of New York at Fredonia. (2023). *Strategic plan 2023: Mission, vision, and goals*. https://bit.ly/41hLdXR

Tualaulelei, E., & Green, N. C. (2023). Supporting educators' professional learning for equity pedagogy: The promise of open educational practices. *Journal for Multicultural Education, 16*(5), 429-442. https://doi.org/nv5n

Vygotsky, L. S. (1978). *Mind in society: The development of higher psychological processes.* Harvard University Press.

Werth, E., & Williams, K. (2023). Learning to be open: Instructor growth through open pedagogy. *Open Learning: The Journal of Open, Distance and e-Learning, 38*(4), 301-314. https://doi.org/gvs9s7

Wesolek, A., Lashley, J., & Langley, A. (2018). *OER: A field guide for academic librarians.* Pacific University Press. https://bit.ly/3CZR75D

Wiley, D., & Hilton III, J. (2018). Defining OER-enabled pedagogy. *The International Review of Research in Open and Distributed Learning, 19*(4), 133-145. https://doi.org/gf6jsr

Chapter 5 Appendix

Appendix A: Faculty OER Survey Example

The following survey instrument was designed at Fredonia to gather insights into faculty engagement with OER. It focuses on teaching practices, perceived benefits and challenges, and the support needed for sustained adoption. This tool can also be adapted by other institutions seeking to assess faculty perceptions and experiences with OER, identify barriers, and inform strategies for promoting broader participation in open education initiatives.

1.   What is your department?
2.   What is your job title?
3.   What types of teaching do you do? (Select all that apply)

    a.   Face-to-Face
    b.   Online recordings
    c.   Live Digital Instruction
    d.   Hybrid

4.   What course(s) are you currently teaching or planning to teach using OER? (Names: Ex., Principles of Accounting, Craft of Writing)
5.   What are these course prefixes: (Ex., ACCT 201, ENGL 100)
6.   Of the courses you are currently teaching or planning to teach using OER, how many sections have you taught and/or are planning to teach?
7.   Have you continued to use OER in course(s) you have previously received a campus OER incentive for?

    a.   Yes
    b.   No
    c.   In some, but not all

8.   If you have stopped using OER for one or more courses, can you explain why? (Select all that apply)

    a.   Lack of support from my institution
    b.   Lack of time
    c.   Too difficult to integrate into technology I use
    d.   Too difficult to use
    e.   Too difficult to change or edit
    f.   Too hard to find what I need
    g.   No comprehensive list

      h. Not enough resources for my subject

      i. Not high-quality

      j. Not effective at improving student performance

      k. Not relevant to my local context

      l. Not knowing if I have permission to change

      m. Not used by other faculty I know

      n. Other:

9. Please list the course title and prefix for any courses you have discontinued the use of OER in:

10. Would you be interested in revisiting the use of OER in this course, if new or better quality resources have become available?

      a. Yes

      b. No

      c. Maybe

11. Which of the following types of support or assistance have you received? (Select all that apply)

      a. Assistance finding content from librarians/PDC

      b. Training opportunities

      c. Technical support

      d. Incentive/stipend

      e. Departmental support

      f. Other:

12. Is there a type of support or assistance not listed that you would like to see?

13. Which OER incentives are you aware of? (Select all that apply)

      a. OER and no-cost adoption incentive

      b. OER textbook creation incentive

      c. Open Pedagogy incentive

      d. Professional development Incentive-OER & OER-enabled pedagogy fellowship

14. What type of campus recognition would you like to see for your work with OER?

15. How would you describe any potential benefits of using OER materials for your students?

16. How would you describe any potential benefits of using OER materials for your teaching?

17. What types of OER materials have you used? (Select all that apply)

      a. Open textbooks

      b. Whole course

      c. Elements of a course (ex. a module/unit)

      d. Videos

e. Podcasts

f. Images

g. Infographics

h. Interactive games

i. Lectures

j. Lesson plans

k. Tutorials

l. Quizzes

m. E-books

n. Data sets

o. Learning tools, instruments and plug-ins

p. Other:

18. Additional Comments (optional): Please add comments here, to help us better understand your course situation and goals.

6. Charting the Future of Open Pedagogy

Angela M. McGowan-Kirsch, PhD

The authors contributing to this book form an innovative community of educators and scholars dedicated to supporting students in developing Open Educational Resources (OER) that promote equalized access to knowledge and educational opportunities worldwide. This book advances educational practices emphasizing critical thinking, cultural sensitivity, and peer-to-peer learning. By promoting the creation and sharing of knowledge, the authors highlight practices that encourage students to take ownership of their learning and foster deeper connections between their coursework and real-world applications.

Drawing on theoretical frameworks and practical examples, the contributing authors demonstrate that OER is not just a tool for cost-saving but a powerful catalyst for making the learning process more active and inclusive. When embracing OER, educators promote new opportunities for collaboration, creativity, and sharing of resources. Aligning with The William and Flora Hewlett Foundation (2013), the authors illustrate OER's transformative potential, which includes:

- equitable access to knowledge, enabling all learners to benefit regardless of socioeconomic status
- lowering the overall financial burden of higher education
- improving learning outcomes
- personalizing educational experiences
- culturally relevant and inclusive instruction by encouraging content adaptation through translation and localization

These benefits exemplify OER's impact on advancing education and reimagining how educators teach and learn.

This book commenced with the goal of exploring how faculty utilize OER and open pedagogy to equip students with the skills they need for active, engaged learning in an evolving educational landscape. As a result, this collection goes beyond conventional academic norms (e.g., assigning disposable assignments, as discussed in Chapter 2) to embrace an approach to teaching and learning that incorporates renewable assignments (e.g., Chapters 3 and 4) and experiments with generative artificial intelligence (e.g., Chapter 5). As the authors illustrate, many disciplines have adopted approaches encouraging student-generated content, which, when shared as open resources, has profoundly influenced teaching and learning (DeRosa & Jhangiani, 2018). These Open Educational Practices (OEP) offer students opportunities to share their work widely, engage in peer review, connect with broader communities, and reflect on their learning (Wiley et al., 2017)—practices central to this book.

A central theme of this book is that open pedagogy should be supported by institutions of higher learning as a means of enhancing skill development by allowing them to contribute to the learning process (see Chapter 5). The authors argue that integrating open pedagogy aids instructors in challenging students intellectually, spurring meaningful engagement with content, and increasing their learning investment. When students take ownership of their education—whether by contributing to course design (Chapter 1), engaging in meaningful discussions (Chapter 3), or applying course concepts to real-world scenarios (Chapter 4)—they engage more actively in their learning. Likewise, Chapters 2 and 3 illuminate how open pedagogy can stimulate critical thinking and assist students with examining the broader relevance of their coursework. The curriculum detailed in this book can be adapted to meet the needs of virtually any high school, undergraduate, or graduate course. To continue the growth of open educational practices and resources, the authors of this text hope to inspire readers to create assessments that generate open access content and share student work publicly under a Creative Commons license.

In using open pedagogy as a dimension of OEP, contributing authors offer techniques that educators can adopt to empower learners to engage with, create, or build on prior OER. Throughout the chapters, it becomes apparent that adopting open pedagogy requires redefining traditional teacher and learner roles, entrusting students to become knowledge producers or curators (DeRosa & Robinson, 2017). Further, open pedagogy redefines teachers as facilitators of learning experiences (DeRosa & Jhangiani, 2018) and democratizes access to knowledge (Casserly & Smith, 2008). To make the transition, instructors must embrace creative endeavors, and students need to be open to these innovative approaches.

Implementing these practices, especially when involving students in OER creation, can pose challenges, such as locating high-quality resources and managing the time-consuming process of content curation (Allen & Seaman, 2016; Petrides et al., 2011). DeRosa and Jhangiani (2017) advocate for faculty to share the barriers, difficulties, and problems that arise when implementing open pedagogy. One such recommendation is that students understand open licenses as a foundational element of co-creating and sharing open resources. Open licenses, such as those provided by Creative Commons, enable students to recognize the legal and ethical dimensions of sharing and reusing content. Instructors can incorporate workshops, interactive tutorials, or other instructional activities focusing on open access guidelines (Baran & AlZoubi, 2020). This approach empowers students and reinforces the principles of transparency underpinning the open education movement (Wiley & Hilton,

2018). Equipping students with a clear understanding of open licenses is an essential practical skill for open content sharing.

A second strategy is designing assessments that promote social justice by facilitating the inclusion of diverse perspectives often overlooked in traditional educational materials. Prompting inclusive education can amplify voices from underrepresented communities (Hodgkinson-Williams & Trotter, 2018) and enable students from marginalized backgrounds to acquire knowledge that reflects their experiences. Chapter 4, in particular, describes an assessment that elevates diversity, equity, and inclusion (DEI) by encouraging students to draw from their cultural experiences, challenge dominant narratives, and contribute content that reflects a broader range of perspectives. These practices strengthen a sense of belonging and enrich open resources with authentic and varied insights. Such approaches demonstrate the transformative potential of open pedagogy in advancing educational equity and promoting social justice in learning environments (Bali et al., 2020). By designing assessments prioritizing inclusivity and social justice, educators, such as those whose work is featured in this book, challenge conventional educational practices, amplify diverse voices, and advocate for a more just educational system.

The authors' works present the importance of OER and open pedagogy in reshaping teaching and learning across disciplines. For example, Hether's Chapter 1 on collaborative syllabus design demonstrates how open pedagogy allows students to take ownership of their learning. This occurs as students contribute to course content and develop renewable assignments that benefit future cohorts (Katz & Van Allen, 2020). Creating and sharing knowledge aligns with broader themes explored in this volume, demonstrating how OER and open pedagogy support sustainability and equitable access to information. For instance, Lohiser's Chapter 3 showcases how a student-developed OER, like observational research projects, can be utilized by future learners in numerous disciplines. She points out that this, in turn, creates a continuous learning cycle (Wiley & Hilton, 2018). Likewise, in Chapter 2, Hertzberg details her students' efforts to work on flow visualization, and Steidinger's Chapter 4 further illustrates how OER and open pedagogy empower students to create publicly accessible resources that transcend the classroom. These practices are essential for building an inclusive and participatory educational ecosystem grounded in collaboration, creativity, and transparency.

Furthermore, Hilburger argues in Chapter 5 that instructors should be supported in integrating open pedagogy. Namely, colleges and universities must provide intentional, ongoing resources that address common barriers instructors experience when implementing open pedagogy and OER. Instructors, for instance, often require time, training, and access to expert resources to feel confident implementing open pedagogy. Institutions can alleviate these challenges by offering structured professional development opportunities and promoting interdisciplinary partnerships among faculty, librarians, and instructional designers. Higher education can empower faculty to create transformative learning experiences by cultivating a culture that values openness and innovation. As Hilburger demonstrates in Chapter

5, an institutional commitment to the open education movement strengthens the adoption of open pedagogy and creates an ecosystem that encourages faculty participation. Additionally, colleges and universities should invest in infrastructure, including accessible repositories for OER and partnerships with libraries and instructional design teams. These efforts support faculty in adopting open pedagogy effectively and fostering a culture of collaboration, innovation, and sustained engagement.

As I conclude this book, a key argument concerns the implications of open pedagogy. The authors establish the transformative power of OER and open pedagogy in reshaping the educational landscape while conveying the importance of involving students as co-creators of knowledge. Although open pedagogy encourages a deeper connection to course content, OER ensures broader access to resources that benefit current and future learners worldwide. Ultimately, this book demonstrates that by embracing OER and open pedagogy, educators can empower students to take ownership of their learning, address real-world issues, and contribute to a global educational community.

References

Allen, I. E., & Seaman, J. (2016). *Opening the textbook: Educational resources in U.S. higher education, 2015-16*. Babson Survey Research Group. http://www.onlinelearningsurvey.com/reports/openingthetextbook2016.pdf

Bali, M., Cronin C., & Jhangiani, R. S. (2020). Framing open educational practices from a social justice perspective. *Journal of Interactive Media in Education, 2020*(1), 1-12. https://doi.org/10.5334/jime.565

Baran, E., & AlZoubi, D. (2020). Affordances, challenges, and impact of open pedagogy: Examining students' voices. *Distance Education, 41*(2), 230-244. https://doi.org/10.1080/01587919.2020.1757409

Casserly, C. M., & Smith, M. S. (2008). Revolutionizing education through innovation: Can openness transform teaching and learning? In T. Iiyoshi & M. S. V. Kumar (Eds.), *Opening up education: The collective advancement of education through open technology, open content, and open knowledge* (pp. 261–275). The MIT Press. https://www.cni.org/wp-content/uploads/2014/07/9780262515016_Open_Access_Edition.pdf

DeRosa, R., & Jhangiani, R. (2018). Open pedagogy. In Rebus Community (Ed.), *A guide to making open textbooks with students*. Pressbooks. https://press.rebus.community/makingopentextbookswithstudents/chapter/open-pedagogy

DeRosa, R., & Robison, S. (2017). From OER to open pedagogy: Harnessing the power of open. In R.S. Jhangiani and R. Biswas-Diener (Eds.), *Open: The philosophy and practices that are revolutionizing education and science* (pp. 115-124). Ubiquity Press. https://doi.org/10.5334/bbc.i

Hodgkinson-Williams, C. A., & Trotter, H. (2018). A social justice framework for understanding Open Educational Resources and practices in the global south. *Journal of Learning for Development, 5*(3), 204-224. https://doi.org/10.56059/jl4d.v5i3.312

Katz, S., & Van Allen, J. (2020). Evolving into the open: A framework for collaborative design of renewable assignments. In A. Clifton & K. D. Hoffman (Eds.), *Open pedagogy approaches: Faculty, library, and student collaborations.* Milne Publishing. https://milnepublishing.geneseo.edu/openpedagogyapproaches/

Petrides, L., Jimes, C., Middleton-Detzner, C., Walling, J., & Weiss, S. (2011). Open textbook adoption and use: Implications for teachers and learners. *Open Learning: The Journal of Open, Distance and e-Learning, 26*(1), 39–49. https://doi.org/10.1080/02680513.2011.538563

The William and Flora Hewlett Foundation. (2013). *Hewlett Foundation 2013 Annual Report.* https://www.hewlett.org/wp-content/uploads/2016/09/2013AnnualReport.pdf

Wiley, D., & Hilton III, J. L. (2018). Defining OER-enabled pedagogy. *The International Review of Research in Open and Distributed Learning, 19*(4), 133-147. https://doi.org/10.19173/irrodl.v19i4.3601

Wiley, D., Webb, A., Weston, S., & Tonks, D. (2017). A preliminary exploration of the relationships between student-created OER, sustainability, and students' success. *The International Review of Research in Open and Distributed Learning, 18*(4), 60-69. https://doi.org/10.19173/irrodl.v18i4.3022

About the Contributors

Editors

Angela M. McGowan-Kirsch, PhD
SUNY FREDONIA

Angela M. McGowan-Kirsch (PhD, The University of Southern Mississippi) is an associate professor of communication at SUNY Fredonia and a recipient of the 2023 Chancellor's Award for Excellence in Teaching. Specializing in rhetoric, communication theory, and political communication, she has completed the Lumen Circles Fellowship in OER-enabled pedagogy. Dr. McGowan-Kirsch is the editor of *Encouraging College Students' Democratic Engagement in an Era of Political Polarization* (Lexington Books, 2025) and has published research in journals such as the *Atlantic Journal of Communication, College Teaching, Journal of the Scholarship of Teaching and Learning* and *Communication Teacher*.

Kelly Soczka Steidinger, M.A.
MID-STATE TECHNICAL COLLEGE & SUNY FREDONIA

Kelly Soczka Steidinger (M.A., Ball State University; M.A., University of Wisconsin-Stevens Point) is a Behavioral Science Instructor at Mid-State Technical College and an Adjunct Communication Lecturer at the State University of New York at Fredonia. She earned an E-Learning and Online Teaching graduate certificate from UW-Stout and completed the Lumen Circles Fellowship in OER-enabled pedagogy. Her research focuses on improving pedagogy, and she has published in *Communication Teacher, College Teaching, Utah Journal of Communication*, and numerous resource books and edited volumes.

Contributors

Christina R. Hilburger, MISt
SUNY FREDONIA

Christina Hilburger (MISt, McGill University) is the Research and Information Literacy Services Librarian at the State University of New York at Fredonia. In addition to providing research support and library instruction, she co-leads Open Fredonia, the campus's open education initiative, where she works closely with faculty to support the discovery, adoption, creation, and evaluation of open educational resources (OER) and advocates for affordable learning solutions for students.

Jean Hertzberg, PhD
UNIVERSITY OF COLORADO, BOULDER

Jean R. Hertzberg (PhD, University of California, Berkeley) is a Professor of Mechanical Engineering at the University of Colorado, Boulder. Her teaching focuses on measurement techniques, thermodynamics, fluid mechanics, and design, and her research interests include vortex-dominated flows. Her recent work includes *Visual Expertise in Fluid Flows: Uncovering a Link Between Conceptual and Perceptual Expertise* (IJEE, 2020). Additional publications are available at jeanbizhertzberg.com.

Heather J. Hether, PhD
UNIVERSITY OF CALIFORNIA, DAVIS

Heather J. Hether (PhD, University of Southern California) is an associate professor of communication at UC Davis. Her research focuses on innovative teaching practices that enhance student learning and prepare students for professional success. She is particularly interested in collaborative and open pedagogy practices that involve students as active co-creators of their educational experiences. Dr. Hether's work has been published in *The Journal of Creative Behavior*, *Health Promotion Practice*, and the *Journal of Health Communication*, as well as in several edited volumes.

Amanda Lohiser, PhD
UNIVERSITY OF ROCHESTER

Amanda Lohiser (PhD, SUNY Buffalo) is a Clinical Assistant Professor of Management Communication at the Simon Business School, University of Rochester. She has taught undergraduate and graduate students in the U.S., Singapore, and Denmark. With a B.A. and Ph.D. in communication studies, an M.S. in public relations, and expertise in creativity and face coding, Dr. Lohiser combines her research and professional experience to foster communication, connection, collaboration, and creativity.

Publisher Acknowledgment

It takes a village to produce an ambitious project such as this; we are deeply grateful for the support and expertise of these generous individuals that worked together to proofread this text:

- Oriana Carletto
- Jennifer DeVito
- Anna Grove
- Pamathi Janakan
- Shruti Mehta
- Allison Richard

www.ingramcontent.com/pod-product-compliance
Lightning Source LLC
Chambersburg PA
CBHW081648270326
41933CB00018B/3383